MEET SAINT FAUSTINA

Herald of Divine Mercy

Meet
SAINT
FAUSTINA

Herald of Divine Mercy

BY REV. GEORGE W. KOSICKI, C.S.B.

SERVANT
BOOKS

PUBLISHED BY ST. ANTHONY MESSENGER PRESS
CINCINNATI, OHIO

Excerpts from the English translation of *Diary of Saint Faustina Kowalska: Divine Mercy in My Soul,* © 1987 Congregation of Marians of the Immaculate Conception. Used by permission. All rights reserved.

Photo of St. Faustina Kowalska © Congregation of Marians of the Immaculate Conception. Used with permission. Extracted from a black-and-white group photo with her family and relatives at her birthplace, Glogowiec (February 1935).Used for the Marian Helpers Bulletin Cover, Spring 2000.

Cover design by Candle Light Studios

Library of Congress Cataloging-In-Publication Data

Kosicki, George W., 1928-
    Meet Saint Faustina : herald of divine mercy / by George W. Kosicki.
        p. cm.
    Includes bibliographical references.
    ISBN 1-56955-236-3 (alk. paper)
    1. Faustina, Saint, 1905-1938. 2. Christian saints—Poland—Biography. I. Title.

BX4700.F175 K67 2001
282'.092—dc21   00-052397

ISBN 1-56955-236-3
Copyright © 2001 by Fr. George Kosicki
All rights reserved.

Published by Servant Books, an imprint of St. Anthony Messenger Press
28 W. Liberty St.
Cincinnati, OH 45202
www.AmericanCatholic.org
Printed in the United States of America

05 06 07 08 09 5 4 3

DEDICATION

To the glory of the merciful heart of Jesus.

CONTENTS

It is obvious that Divine Providence was preparing my dear friend, Fr. George Kosicki, to write on St. Faustina and the whole Divine Mercy Devotion when his mother was asked by some Marian priests to paint the image only a few years after the saint's death. This book represents the newest and most comprehensive of Fr. George's many efforts to spread devotion to the Divine Mercy. Even those familiar with the history and meaning of this devotion will learn much from *Meet St. Faustina*. Fr. George develops a number of new areas of interest like the relationship of Eastern spirituality to the experience and insights of St. Faustina. He also explains the painful misunderstanding and disapproval of this devotion early on, as well as the gradual changes in attitude motivated largely by the archbishop of Krakow who became Pope John Paul II.

Best of all are Fr. George's own discussions of the spiritual teachings contained in the diary and life of St. Faustina. The various Christian schools and movements of spirituality do not differ essentially from each other since all are based on the Gospels themselves. All these approaches to the spiritual journey are examined and guided by Tradition and the Church. However, there are different emphases in each or at least different ways of expressing key ideas. It is these differences that enrich the vast library of Catholic spiritual literature. This book focuses on the special emphasis of the Divine Mercy devotion, especially the meaning and depth of God's mercy and the necessary complete trust and confidence that this mercy summons forth from the human heart and soul.

Anyone familiar with the history of mysticism will have to smile at the familiar pattern of God's preferences—He exalts the lowly *again*. St. Faustina, with her two winters of education and her trying spiritual preparation, as well as her premature difficult death, brings to mind a whole line of simple, devout, intensely dedicated, and humble young women whom God has chosen to be prophetesses in His Church. Beginning with martyrs like Agnes, Catherine, and Lucy, the history of the Church has a remarkable line of young women to whom were revealed the mysteries of the kingdom of God. One thinks immediately of Joan of Arc, who brought an end to the Hundred Years' War and saved her homeland for the Catholic faith by being docile to the heavenly voices. Then there is the great Catherine of Siena, whose visions historically saved the papacy. There is a whole line of visionary women who have shaped Catholic devotion in modern times: Margaret Mary, Bernadette, Catherine Labouré, and the children of Fatima—all of these are "the little ones" that Jesus has spoken to. Although not a visionary in the sense of the others, one cannot fail to mention how the Holy Spirit has affected the history of the Church by that other young woman who died so painfully, Thérèse of Lisieux.

Parenthetically, it is worthwhile to remember that the teachings of the Church on private revelations, even those given to canonized saints, indicate that they do not have the authority or inerrancy of Sacred Scripture. Private revelations always reflect the personal experience of the individual who has received these special graces. Their visions and messages are colored by their knowledge and their own personal thoughts and understanding of the visions they received. It is important to keep in mind that any of these revelations given by the Holy Spirit to the Church at a particular time are really encounters of the finite with the Infinite. Visionaries are apparently chosen because they will be docile and honest, and will avoid controversy. They cannot, however, avoid including their own ideas in the description of what they experience, even when they do their very best to be objective.

Only a visionary like St. Bernadette, who received a very simple and brief message, can keep his or her ideas to a bare minimum.

Probably many of the visions of St. Faustina fall into the category that St. John of the Cross calls intellectual visions. In this case, the mind of the individual under the inspiration of grace seeks adequate forms and words to express the truths he or she experiences. It's obvious, for example, that any vision of the Holy Trinity must be like this because no human can perceive the infinity of God. One can perceive this personal quality of intellectual visions in St. Faustina's fascinating description of her Trinitarian experience. I have tried to explore some of these profound and mysterious concepts in my book *A Still Small Voice*—a review of the Church's teaching on private revelation (Ignatius Press). When we understand as much as we can about this profoundly mysterious topic of private revelations and visions, we are far better prepared to learn from them. We can avoid a kind of fundamentalism and excessive literalism that can cause trouble even with the interpretation of the Holy Scripture, which is public revelation.

The spiritual doctrine and meaning of Divine Mercy, which is communicated so effectively to the pure and suffering soul of St. Faustina, is well summed up by Fr. George. Of course, he is guided in this by the magnificent encyclical on Divine Mercy by Pope John Paul II. The diary of St. Faustina can be an awesome document to approach because of its length, complexity, and mysterious origins as private revelation. In this book the content and meaning of the diary are very effectively analyzed and related to the present situation in the Church as well as in world history.

This is a book to keep for a long time. You may want to have your own personal copy so that you can write marginal notes and underline. You will also want to share copies with friends who are sincerely seeking to grow in the love of God and

Christian discipleship. It can also be shared with Christians of other denominations, especially Eastern Orthodox friends. This book may be the source of a special grace to the large number of people returning to the Church now who are troubled by the memory of the years when they were off the track. The mystery of Divine Mercy is an essential and most powerful element in the Christian life. Here you will find it very well explored through the life and experiences of the great and humble mystic of our times.

Fr. Benedict J. Groeschel, CFR

Helena Kowalska was born in the little rural village of Glogowiec, Poland, in the year 1905. As early as the age of seven, she heard the voice of the Lord in her soul, calling her to a more perfect way of life. As a result, just before her twentieth birthday, with hardly a penny to her name and without her parents' permission, she journeyed alone by rail to Warsaw to pursue a call to the religious life. A year later, she entered the convent of the Sisters of Our Lady of Mercy.

Over the next few years, Sr. Maria Faustina of the Most Blessed Sacrament (Helena's chosen religious name) deepened her life of prayer and grew strong in her practice of Christian virtues. She regularly performed the most menial tasks for her community: as cook, gardener, and portress, for example. But she was noted especially for her cheerfulness, for her care for the poor who came to the convent seeking food, and for her loving kindness to the girls whom the sisters trained and educated at their houses. In fact, many of the sisters knew of her desire for holiness, and so they trusted her and came to her for counsel and advice—so much so that she earned the nickname "the dump," because they were always "dumping" their problems on her.

After an intense period of spiritual purification that occurred early in her life as a religious, Our Lord brought her into a special intimacy with His merciful Heart. She began to receive mystical revelations, visions, locutions, and prophecies, all focused on the same theme: the Mercy of the Lord for the lost and the broken. At the command of her spiritual director, she recorded her spiritual experiences in her diary, which is now regarded as an outstanding spiritual classic of the twentieth century and a miracle in itself, given that Sr. Faustina had barely two winters of elementary education!

Sr. Faustina also bore many sufferings: from the tuberculosis which gradually ravaged her body, to the uncharitable misinterpretation of her growing physical weakness by many of her fellow sisters, to her anguish about her own seeming inability to carry out the Lord's requests to her. He had asked her to initiate several forms of devotion to His Divine Mercy throughout the world, that a wayward and wounded mankind—already headed for a second world war—might soon learn to ask for His Mercy, completely trust in His Mercy, and be merciful to others, as He is merciful.

Sr. Faustina offered up all her prayers, works, and sufferings, in union with the crucified Jesus, for mercy upon poor sinners, especially those who have lost their trust in God's goodness. In addition, our Lord frequently appeared to her as a child, asking her to learn from Him the lesson of spiritual childhood: to approach God with humility and trust, as a little child would do. These themes of her spiritual life echo the "little way" of another great mystic of modern times, St. Thérèse of Lisieux.

St. Faustina died on October 5, 1938, but her mission was far from over. In fact, it was only just beginning. She wrote: "I feel certain that my mission will not come to an end upon my death, but will begin. O doubting souls, I will draw aside the veils of heaven to convince you of God's goodness" (*Diary*, 281). By her heavenly intercessions, St. Faustina has been fulfilling that promise ever since, obtaining countless graces and miracles for suffering souls from the compassionate Heart of Jesus:

O my Jesus, each of Your saints reflects one of Your virtues; I desire to reflect Your compassionate heart, full of mercy; I want to glorify it. Let Your mercy, O Jesus, be impressed upon my heart and soul like a seal, and this will be my badge in this and the future life. Glorifying Your mercy is the exclusive task of my life. (*Diary,* 1242)

Perhaps the message and mission of St. Faustina to the modern world was best summed up by the Holy Father, Pope John Paul II, in his homily for her beatification on Divine Mercy Sunday, April 18, 1993:

Her mission continues and is yielding astonishing fruit. It is truly marvelous how her devotion to the merciful Jesus is spreading in our contemporary world and gaining so many human hearts! This is doubtlessly a sign of the times—a sign of our twentieth century. The balance of this century which is now ending ... presents a deep restlessness and fear of the future. Where, if not in the Divine Mercy, can the world find refuge and the light of hope? Believers understand that perfectly.

Rev. Seraphim Michalenko, MIC
Vice-Postulator of the
Cause for the Canonization of St. Faustina,
and Director Emeritus of
the John Paul II Institute of Divine Mercy

ACKNOWLEDGMENT

Special thanks to Christine Kruszyna, the "secretary of Divine Mercy" (see *Diary,* 965) who faithfully over the years read my handwriting and meticulously transcribed it onto the computer disk.

I want to tell you about my favorite saint, who is important not only to me but to the Church of the third millennium. In religious life she is called Sr. Faustina. Her full religious name is Sr. Maria Faustina of the Most Blessed Sacrament.

I first came to know of her in the early 1940s, when Marian priests living in my home parish asked my mother to paint an image of Sr. Faustina's vision of the merciful Jesus. However, my mother's specialty was not portrait painting, and her attempt was not satisfactory. Nevertheless, in 1946, when I entered my religious community, she gave me a framed print of the merciful Jesus done in Mexico, with the words Jezu ufam Tobie! ("Jesus, I trust in You" in Polish). It has hung above my bed for over a half century.

It wasn't until 1985, during an extended hermitage retreat, that I felt called to proclaim full-time God's mercy according to the revelations of Sr. Faustina. This I did through continued study, writing, and preaching.

In the fall of 1992, while at the Shrine of Sr. Faustina in Lagiewniki (suburb of Krakow) as chaplain for a Divine Mercy pilgrimage to Poland, I came to know her in a more personal way. Our tour bus was ready to depart, but two pilgrims were missing. I anxiously went back into the shrine, looking for them, and as I passed by the tomb of Sr. Faustina I heard in my heart: "I am your sister, trust even more!" These words stayed with me for the rest of the pilgrimage and for weeks afterward. I printed them out on three-by-five index cards and put them at the door of my house, at the entrance to the chapel, and on the bathroom mirror.

Trust Even More!

To trust in Jesus is the heart of the life and spirituality of St. Faustina. In this book, *Meet Saint Faustina: Herald of Divine Mercy*, I will introduce you to her life and spirituality—which I call "The Merciful Way." I will also tell you about Pope John Paul II's personal involvement in the Divine Mercy message and devotion, and how he was influenced by the life and mission of Sr. Faustina. The life and mission of St. Faustina fulfills the challenge of John Paul II to the Church of the third millennium: to be holy, to evangelize, and to be committed to church unity. Also included are excerpts of some of St. Faustina's prayers. A bibliography will help those interested to find more material on this important saint of the new millennium.

The Divine Mercy message and devotion is an urgent message for the whole world to hear and act upon. Pope John Paul II cried out to the world at the beatification of Sr. Faustina:

Where, if not in the Divine Mercy, can the world find refuge and the light of hope?

And at the Shrine of Divine Mercy in Poland he proclaimed:

There is nothing that mankind needs more than Divine Mercy.

It is my prayer that this book will help you to meet St. Faustina, who is the Apostle of Divine Mercy, and help you become a witness of that mercy to our world.

CHAPTER 1

The Life of St. Faustina
From Farm to Convent: 1905–30

Born in the Heart of Poland

Faustina was born in the small village of Glogowiec, Poland, near Lodz, on August 25, 1905. Two days later, Stanislaus Kowalski and his wife Marianna took their third child to nearby Swinice, where she was baptized "Helena" in the parish church of St. Casimir. One of ten children of a poor farmer and carpenter, she knew what it was to live simply in a small cottage, doing chores around the house and working on the farm. She and her sisters took turns attending Mass on Sundays, sharing the one good dress they owned.

Religion was central to the Kowalski family. Stanislaus sang out his daily prayers early in the morning before work. While his daughter was young, he taught her short prayers and how to read the lives of saints and missionaries. Helen, as she was called by her family, was a gifted storyteller. She fascinated other children by repeating the stories to them. Her mother's tender compassion and dedication to husband and family also influenced her.

Unusually drawn to spiritual pursuits, Helen was seven when she first heard a voice in her soul challenging her to a more perfect way of life (*Diary*, 7). At the age of nine she received her first Holy Communion.

Since Polish schools had been closed during the Russian occupation, Helen did not begin her primary education until age twelve. Her schooling was cut off after two winters when officials decided to make room for younger students.

In the spring of 1921, in order to assist her parents, she went to work as a housemaid and baby-sitter in the town of Alexandrow. Her joyful spirit and natural gift of storytelling, combined with innate skill in nurturing children, made her a favorite. Helen, however, was still drawn to a more spiritual life. After a year, she returned home and informed her parents that she wanted to join a convent. Neither paid attention to her pleas.

In the fall of 1922, Helen left home again, this time to work in Lodz. Her prayer life deepened, and she disciplined herself by fasting. The families she worked for were delighted with her goodness, helpfulness, and joyous laughter.

The Turning Point

In July of 1924 she and her sister, Josephine, attended a dance in the park behind the Cathedral of St. Stanislaus in Lodz. There, she suddenly saw Jesus at her side. He was racked with pain, stripped of his clothing, and covered with wounds. He spoke to her: **How long shall I put up with you, and how long will you keep putting Me off?** (*Diary*, 9).

This was the turning point in her life. She ran to the cathedral, threw herself on the floor before the altar, and begged the Lord to be good enough to let her know what she should do next (*Diary*, 9). Then she heard these words: **Go at once to Warsaw; you will enter a convent there** (*Diary*, 10).

Helen went home and packed her things. When morning came she said good-bye to her sister and uncle, who then took her to the train for Warsaw. Obedient to the word she had heard, and with only the clothes on her back, Helen set off for the city.

In Warsaw she knew no one. After morning Mass, a priest directed her to a woman who would help with a place to stay.

Helen began her search for a convent to enter, but none would accept her until she knocked at the door of the Sisters of Our Lady of Mercy. The Mother Superior took a liking to Helen and told her to go to the Lord of the house and ask whether He would accept her. With joy she went to the chapel and asked the Lord Jesus, "Do you accept me?" She immediately heard: **I do accept you; you are in My heart.** On returning to Mother Superior, who asked, "Well, has the Lord accepted you?" Helen answered, "Yes." "If the Lord has accepted," Mother responded, "then I also will accept" (see *Diary*, 14).

Because Helen had no money for a sister's wardrobe, Mother suggested she continue working and set aside the needed funds. Helen regularly delivered her earnings to the convent. Within a year she had enough. Helen Kowalska finally entered the convent, becoming a postulant on the eve of the Feast of Our Lady of the Angels, August 1, 1925. Later she wrote:"I felt immensely happy; it seemed to me that I had stepped into the life of Paradise. A single prayer was bursting forth from my heart, one of thanksgiving" (*Diary*, 17).

Life Is Full of Struggles

But within three weeks she was tempted to see Mother Superior and leave the community. The lack of time for prayer and the busy work schedule made Helen consider joining a stricter order. But the Lord intervened with a vision of His face in agony. Helen asked, "Jesus, who has hurt you so?" And Jesus answered, **It is you who will cause Me this pain if you leave this convent. It is to this place that I called you and nowhere else; and I have prepared many graces for you** (*Diary*, 19).

During her first year at the convent, Helen's health began to decline, and the Superior sent her away for a rest. Later, along with the other postulants, Helen went to Krakow where the order ran a large institution for wayward girls. There she finished the remaining three months of her postulancy and prepared to enter the novitiate.

Her Years as a Novice

On April 30, 1926, Helen received the habit and veil and her new name, Sr. Maria Faustina of the Most Blessed Sacrament. Later she wrote of the experience in her diary: "The day I took the [religious] habit, God let me understand how much I was to suffer. I clearly saw to what I was committing myself. I experienced a moment of that suffering. But then God filled my soul again with great consolations" (*Diary*, 22).

In Krakow, Sr. Faustina began her two novitiate years of formal training in the work and spiritual life of the community. She was popular with the other novices. Faustina's good nature, willingness to defer to others for the sake of Jesus, and enlightening conversations drew them to her. Toward the end of her first year, she began to experience some of the suffering and struggle that became part of her life and mission. Finding neither joy nor consolation in prayer, and increasingly aware of her own sinfulness, she entered into a dark night of the soul:

> Toward the end of the first year of my novitiate, darkness began to cast its shadow over my soul. I felt no consolation in prayer; I had to make a great effort to meditate; fear began to sweep over me. Going deeper into myself, I could find nothing but great misery. I could also clearly see the great holiness of God. I did not dare to raise my eyes to Him, but reduced myself to dust under His feet and begged for mercy.... The simple truths of the faith became incomprehensible to me. My soul was in anguish, unable to find comfort anywhere.
>
> At a certain point, there came to me the very powerful

impression that I am rejected by God. This terrible thought pierced my soul right through; in the midst of the suffering my soul began to experience the agony of death. I wanted to die but could not.... When I made this known to the Directress of Novices, I received this reply, "Know, dear Sister, that God has chosen you for great sanctity. This is a sign that God wants to have you very close to Himself in Heaven. Have great trust in the Lord Jesus." (*Diary*, 23)

Faustina's response to this dark night gives us the key to her spirituality and mission in the church:

During these terrible moments I said to God, "Jesus, who in the Gospel compare Yourself to a most tender mother, I trust in Your words because You are Truth and Life. In spite of everything, Jesus, I trust in You in the face of every interior sentiment which sets itself against hope. Do what You want with me; I will never leave You, because You are the source of my life." (*Diary*, 24)

Near the end of her novitiate, Faustina's interior sufferings were accompanied by physical weaknesses. The Mother Directress excused her from the customary spiritual disciplines and suggested that Faustina replace them with short prayers. On Good Friday 1928, Faustina wrote of her experience as she prayed:

Jesus catches up my heart into the very flame of His love. This was during the evening adoration. All of a sudden, the Divine Presence invaded me, and I forgot everything else. Jesus gave me to understand how much He had suffered for me. This lasted a very short time. An intense yearning—a longing to love God. (*Diary*, 26)

First Vows

Sr. Faustina's novitiate ended on April 30, 1928 when she made simple vows for one year. The dark night lingered for six more months. Through these sufferings, Faustina grew into a deeper love of the Lord and awareness of her own misery and God's mercy. She wrote:

> At the beginning of my religious life, suffering and adversities frightened and disheartened me. So I prayed continuously, asking Jesus to strengthen me and to grant me the power of His Holy Spirit that I might carry out His holy will in all things, because from the beginning I have been aware of my weakness.... The knowledge of my own misery allows me, at the same time, to know the immensity of Your mercy. In my own interior life, I am looking with one eye at the abyss of my misery and baseness, and with the other, at the abyss of Your mercy, O God. (*Diary*, 56)

Six months after making her simple vows, Faustina was moved to the convent in Warsaw where she had begun her journey into religious life. After just a month of kitchen duty, she became ill and was sent to the infirmary. At this time and throughout much of her life, Faustina suffered not only physically and from her interior struggle but also from harsh treatment by those around her. Many did not believe she was sick but thought she was pretending in order to avoid the rigors of religious life. The distrust and gossip pained her deeply.

Mother Michael, who had admitted Faustina years ago and who had since been elected Superior General of the community, told her: "Sister, along your path, sufferings just spring up out of the ground. I look upon you, Sister, as one crucified. But I can see that Jesus has a hand in this. Be faithful to the Lord" (*Diary*, 149).

Faustina remained faithful through the dull routine of her jobs as she was moved from house to house. She was sometimes cook or gardener, and a porter when she was too ill for physical work. In her diary, she reflected on the blessings that even monotonous work could bring:

O life so dull and monotonous, how many treasures you contain! When I look at everything with the eyes of faith, no two hours are alike, and the dullness and monotony disappear. The grace which is given me in this hour will not be repeated in the next. (*Diary*, 62)

Because of her ready and agreeable nature, Faustina was a blessing to her superiors. They could send her wherever a need arose. They were unaware of her chronic tubercular condition that was aggravated by their demanding assignments.

In June 1930, Sr. Faustina was sent to Plock and Guardian Angel Home, where she was again assigned to kitchen duty. After a few months, the work became too physically demanding. Faustina was sent to the sisters' rest home in Biala, where she remained for the rest of the year. Once she felt better, she returned to Guardian Angel Home to work in the bakery and store. Plock would remain her home until she returned to Warsaw to prepare for perpetual vows in November 1932.

Throughout her years at Plock, Faustina was continually afflicted by illness and spiritual torment. She had found no spiritual director, and her confessors were often unable to help her. Many of her companions thought her strange. The doubts of others sowed doubt in her own heart. However, whenever she spoke to Jesus about her uncertainty or her inability to go on, he reassured her: **Do not fear; I am with you** (*Diary*, 129). In God's plan this suffering and doubt perfected her trust and the obedience necessary for a mission far more demanding.

Devotions of Divine Mercy (1930–38)

The Image of the Divine Mercy

The mission of St. Faustina began with a revelation on February 22, 1931, in the convent in Plock. She wrote:

> In the evening, when I was in my cell, I saw the Lord Jesus clothed in a white garment. One hand [was] raised in the gesture of blessing, the other was touching the garment at the breast. From beneath the garment, slightly drawn aside at the breast, there were emanating two large rays, one red, the other pale. In silence I kept my gaze fixed on the Lord; my soul was struck with awe, but also with great joy. After a while, Jesus said to me, **Paint an image according to the pattern you see, with the signature: Jesus, I trust in You. I desire that this image be venerated, first in your chapel, and [then] throughout the world.** (*Diary*, 47)

> **I promise that the soul that will venerate this image will not perish. I also promise victory over [its] enemies already here on earth, especially at the hour of death. I Myself will defend it as My own glory.** (*Diary*, 48)

This was the first major revelation of the Divine Mercy to Sr. Faustina. Through it, Jesus made known his great desire that all come to the rays of mercy, all come to His heart, pierced for us and flowing with blood and water (Jn 19:34).

Some time later, her spiritual director and confessor, Fr. Michael Sopocko, asked Sr. Faustina to ask the Lord Jesus the meaning of the two rays in the image. Obediently, she recorded His response:

During prayer I heard these words within me: **The two rays denote Blood and Water. The pale ray stands for the Water which makes souls righteous. The red ray stands for the Blood which is the life of souls....**

These two rays issued forth from the very depths of My tender mercy when My agonized Heart was opened by a lance on the Cross.

These rays shield souls from the wrath of My Father. Happy is the one who will dwell in their shelter, for the just hand of God shall not lay hold of him. (*Diary,* 299)

The Feast

Her first revelation was immediately followed by another major request by Our Lord for a Feast of Mercy:

When I told this to my confessor, I received this for a reply: "That refers to your soul." He told me, "Certainly, paint God's image in your soul." When I came out of the confessional, I again heard words such as these: **My image already is in your soul. I desire that there be a Feast of Mercy. I want this image, which you will paint with a brush, to be solemnly blessed on the first Sunday after Easter; that Sunday is to be the Feast of Mercy.** (*Diary,* 49)

I desire that priests proclaim this great mercy of Mine towards souls of sinners. Let the sinner not be afraid to approach Me. The flames of mercy are burning Me—clamoring to be spent; I want to pour them out upon these souls. (*Diary,* 50)

Soon after these revelations Faustina suffered increased derision from the sisters. She bore them in silence. The humiliations and suffering increased. Confused, she sometimes tried to ignore the inspirations by giving her attention more completely to tasks at hand. She prayed for a spiritual director to help her discern God's movement within her soul.

Preparing for Final Vows

In November 1932, Faustina returned to Warsaw to begin her third probation and to prepare for her perpetual vows. Shortly after arriving, the Mother Directress sent her to a retreat in Walendow. Jesus assured Faustina that during the retreat He would remove her doubts regarding His commands. This was accomplished through the words of Rev. Edmund Elter, S.J., the retreat master. During her confession, Faustina was reassured that God was the source of her inspirations. Fr. Elter encouraged her to pray for a spiritual director. Meanwhile, he said, she was to remain faithful to Jesus despite the hardships that would bring to her.

On December 1, 1932, her third probation began. During this year, she continued to have visions and conversations with Jesus in her heart. He was preparing Faustina to make an offering of herself in atonement for the sins of the world. He made it clear to her that she would suffer and that He waited for her free consent. She recorded this in her diary:

Once during an adoration, the Lord demanded that I give myself up to Him as an offering, by bearing a certain suffering in atonement, not only for the sins of the world in general, but specifically for transgressions committed in this house. Immediately I said, "Very good; I am ready." But Jesus gave me to see what I was going to suffer, and in one moment the whole passion unfolded itself before my eyes.... All these things stood before my soul's eye like a dark storm from which lightning was ready to strike at any moment, waiting only for my consent. For a moment, my nature was frightened. Then suddenly the dinner bell rang. I left the chapel, trembling and undecided. But the sacrifice was ever present before me, for I had neither decided to accept it, nor had I refused the Lord. I wanted to place myself completely in His will. If the Lord Jesus Himself were to impose it on me, I was ready. But Jesus gave me to know that I myself was to give my free consent and accept it with full consciousness, or else it would be meaningless. Its whole power was contained in my free act before God.... And so I then answered immediately, "Jesus, I accept everything that You wish to send me; I trust in Your goodness." At that moment, I felt that by this act I glorified God greatly. But I armed myself with patience. As soon as I left the chapel, I had an encounter with reality. I do not want to describe the details, but there was as much of it as I was able to bear. (*Diary,* 190)

During Lent, Faustina received the stigmata. She suffered internally from the wounds of Jesus. While no outward sign of Jesus' wounds was present, she felt the agony of them in her hands, feet, and side. This suffering and union with the passion of Jesus occurred many times throughout her professed life. Since nothing was outwardly visible, only she and her confessor were aware of it. The Mother Directress Margaret, who recognized that God was calling Faustina to deep union, was a great support to her. Still haunted by doubts, Faustina received Jesus' promise that he would give her help during the retreat before her final profession.

The retreat began on April 17, at St. Joseph's in Krakow. The help came from Fr. Joseph Andrasz, S.J. On the fourth day of the retreat, Faustina confessed to Fr. Andrasz and asked him to release her from her inner visions and the responsibilities they brought. He would not, but affirmed her visions and asked her to pray for a permanent spiritual director. Faustina did pray, and she received a vision of her future spiritual director.

Final Vows
On May 1, 1933, Faustina made her perpetual vows as a sister in the Congregation of the Sisters of Mercy. Her joy was beyond expression. In her diary she wrote that she was nervous about leaving the novitiate and the ever watchful care of Mother Directress. Faustina told Jesus that she would enter his novitiate and remain forever "The little novice of Jesus" (*Diary*, 228).

After her profession she was sent to Vilnius where she was to become head gardener. With little knowledge of gardening, she trusted God to help her in her work. She was hesitant to leave Fr. Andrasz, but Jesus assured her: "Do not fear. I will not leave you alone." When she arrived on May 25, 1933, she found a place quite different than St. Joseph's. The convent consisted of a few small huts occupied by eighteen sisters. Here at last she found her spiritual director, Rev. Michael Sopocko. She recognized him from her vision. He was sensitive to her deep spirituality from the first and remained so for the rest of her life. At his direction, she began to write her now famous diary.

During her three years at Vilnius, Faustina remained cheerful, obedient, and patient. The garden thrived and those with whom she worked noted her saintly behavior.

After Faustina told Fr. Sopocko about Jesus' desire to have the image of her vision of him painted, he arranged for a local artist, Eugene Kazimierowski, to do the work. It was begun on January 2, 1934. Every two weeks Faustina went to him and directed the painting. It was completed in June of that year.

Faustina grew in wisdom and in her love of God. On Holy

Thursday, March 29, 1934, Jesus spoke to her, and she responded with an offering of prayer:

> Jesus said to me, **I desire that you make an offering of yourself for sinners and especially for those souls who have lost hope in God's mercy.** (*Diary*, 308)

In her prayer "God and Souls: Act of Oblation," Faustina offered herself to God for the conversion of sinners, especially those who had lost hope in God's mercy.

After having made this prayer with the permission of Fr. Sopocko, Sr. Faustina felt immediate results. Her soul "became like a stone—dried up, filled with torment and disquiet"(*Diary*, 311). Still, she accepted all as God's will. The Lord brought Sr. Faustina to a total trust in Him.

Her year continued as usual, filled with work and prayer and punctuated by illness. In August she suffered her first violent attack of asthma. This may have resulted from the tuberculosis that already plagued her and would cause almost constant suffering for the rest of her life. She continued to have visions of Jesus. In her diary she recorded experiences and conversations with Him. When she experienced spiritual dryness, as she did during Advent of that year, He reassured her with words of encouragement and a sense of peace.

In February 1935, having received news of her mother's impending death and her wish to see her daughter one last time, Faustina received permission to visit her family. She had not been home for ten years. Faustina arrived and went directly to her mother. After greeting her with the words, "Praised be Jesus Christ," and assuring Faustina that she would be "up and about," her mother sat up in bed. While her doctors had told her she could not improve without surgery, Faustina's mother was well. In fact, she lived to be ninety!

Friends and neighbors filled the house and brought their children for Faustina to hold and kiss. The guests enjoyed hearing her tell stories of the saints and speak of God. While she enjoyed the visit and gave thanks for the opportunity to see her family again, she missed solitude and prayer. On her return to the convent, Jesus assured her that her time with her family had been pleasing to him.

During Lent, Jesus revealed to her that the Image of Divine Mercy should be publicly displayed. Despite his doubts about being able to arrange it, and at considerable personal expense, Fr. Sopocko had the painting displayed in a prominent window of the Ostra Brama (the Shrine of Our Lady of Mercy in Vilnius). He preached there at the three-day celebration at the end of the Jubilee Year of Redemption, 1935. This first display of the Image fell on the Feast of Divine Mercy.

Faustina soon received a message from Jesus that would trouble her for most of her remaining years: He asked that she leave her congregation and begin a new community. Time after time she asked her spiritual director and her confessors about this. Each time she was told to wait, or not to do anything without the consent of her superiors. Faustina loved her community and was not eager to leave it. However, she would do anything if she knew it was God's will.

The Chaplet

In September 1935, God revealed to her a powerful prayer for mercy on the whole world: the Chaplet of Divine Mercy. Said on the beads of the rosary, the prayer pleads for God's mercy on the world, offering Him the sacrifice of His beloved Son, Jesus Christ. Later, Fr. Sopocko had this prayer printed on a card with the Image of Divine Mercy reproduced on the opposite side.

The chaplet, the Act of Oblation, the abandonment to God's will, the stigmata, and her close identification with Jesus' passion all point to Faustina's role in the Church. On September 30, Faustina wrote in her diary that she was sure of her mission to the Church and the world: She was to spend her life pleading for mercy for the world.

How that would be accomplished she was not sure. During her October retreat in Krakow she asked her confessor, Fr. Andrasz, about forming the new community. Again, he advised against doing anything at that time. He felt Faustina's perpetual vows were a sign that God wanted her to remain in her present congregation. If she remained faithful to God and obedient to her superiors, Fr. Andrasz reassured her, the Lord would not allow her to fall into error. In later visions, Jesus also comforted her. His will would be done. She should not worry about how it would come about.

Try as she might, Faustina could not put worry over the new community out of her heart. On one hand, it seemed that Jesus was telling her to begin something new. On the other, her superiors and confessors continued to discourage immediate action. This spiritual turmoil affected her physical health. She approached the archbishop of Vilnius, Romuald Jalbrzykowski, at the beginning of 1936 to ask his guidance. He added his voice to the others: Wait.

After a visit to Warsaw in March 1936, Faustina accepted a new assignment to a convent in Walendow. The convent was financially unstable, and the sisters were required to work long hours. Despite her poor health, Faustina was assigned difficult tasks. Her health worsened, and in late April she was sent to Derdy, a country home for girls. Located in the forest near Walendow, it provided Faustina a place to rest and pray. However, her health continued to decline. On May 11 she was returned to Warsaw, where she would be closer to doctors.

Faustina continued to have visions and conversations with Jesus. Her physical and spiritual sufferings increased, but she bore them with patience and love. Joining her sufferings to the sufferings of Jesus was her way of obtaining mercy for souls and for the world.

In September Blessed Mary appeared to her and asked her to pray especially for Poland. Also in this month Faustina received a message about the Feast of Divine Mercy. Jesus told her that He desired it to be celebrated on the first Sunday after Easter. On that day he would pour out an "ocean of graces" (*Diary*, 699). He promised complete forgiveness of sins and of punishment to anyone who would go to confession and receive Communion on that feast.

Faustina faithfully recorded all Jesus said to her. Her suffering increased and at the end of the month her illness was diagnosed as tuberculosis. She was separated from the other sisters to avoid spreading the disease. However, she still had chores to do.

On her October retreat, she experienced union with God and had a vision of hell. She was also told explicit ways to worship the mercy of God: First, she must show mercy, which grows from love of God, to all neighbors. Then, she was to show mercy in three ways: in deed, word, and prayer.

Her Illness Worsens

Finally, in December of 1936, Faustina was sent to the sanatorium in Pradnik, near Krakow, for three months of treatments. She had a private room and was treated with great kindness. As sick as she was, Faustina found strength to minister to other sick and dying patients. Sometimes she would waken in the night, knowing that someone was near death and in need of prayer. As Jesus had instructed her, she prayed the Chaplet of Divine

Mercy, obtaining for the person a peaceful death and the unlimited mercy of God.

Much to her delight, Faustina was permitted to return home to her convent to celebrate Christmas. She enjoyed her few days with her community, but by December 27, she was back at the sanatorium.

When the new year 1937 arrived, Faustina resolved to do all she could to grow in holiness and attain union with God. She tried to do what she imagined He would do in every situation. Jesus assured her that above all she must love her neighbor and think first of others. As time went on, Faustina felt less at home on earth and longed for the day when she would be united with her Lord for eternity.

Lent was a time of special graces for Faustina. On Good Friday she was completely immersed in the Trinity. On Holy Saturday she was able to return to the convent in Lagiewniki, near Krakow. There Jesus appeared to her at Easter Mass.

However, despite her growing union with God and the many graces she received, Faustina remained concerned about her inability to complete the work of God that she felt called to do: begin a new community. When the Mother General visited the convent to receive the sisters' vows, Faustina asked her again about leaving. Mother told her that whatever she chose to do, she could do. When Faustina left the meeting a feeling of great darkness wrapped itself about her. When she confided that to Mother General, she was told that her desire to leave was a great temptation. Faustina called this dilemma an "endless agony of the soul" (*Diary*, 1116).

Throughout the spring and summer, Faustina continued to record Jesus' words to her. She was told that we most resemble God when we forgive one another. God is Love, Mercy, and Goodness. She found following Jesus difficult, but never lost her desire to be a mirror of her beloved Lord.

At the end of July Faustina was moved to Rabka, a village in the Carpathian Mountains. There she stayed in a rest home for girls and sisters. Her lungs were excruciatingly painful, and her health continued to worsen. She was visited with visions of Mary, Joseph, and St. Barbara. On August 10 she returned to Krakow, where she wrote down the Novena to the Divine Mercy. Fr. Sopocko visited her at the end of the month and told her that work on establishing a Feast of Divine Mercy was going well, as were his efforts to spread the chaplet, litany, and novena.

At Mass on the first Friday of September, having made a prayer of total abandonment to God's will, Faustina had reached a stage of holy indifference. She trusted in God completely, willing to accept whatever He required of her.

Much suffering was in store for her. Despite physical agony, Faustina still had assigned duties at the convent. Only Jesus knew the effort required to perform them. Another source of anguish came from the unkindnesses and suspicions of those with whom she lived. Her life was a confirmation of the letter she received from Fr. Sopocko: God required prayer and sacrifice from her. Her work would be suffering, not the action of forming a new community.

Her Final Year

Her last year, 1938, began as the old one had ended: with physical and spiritual pain. She welcomed the new year, however, and all it would bring. She saw its increased suffering as more opportunities to love God and save souls. Since Jesus had revealed to her the day of her death, she knew that it, too, was coming in the new year. She was more than ready to embrace it.

In her bleakest times Jesus consoled her, saying that He was with her, even when she could not feel His presence. She continued to write and to accept without complaining the cruel treatment she received from those who were her caretakers. The year was filled with times of darkness when she was confused and had to make a willful choice to believe.

During this time, as in every part of her life, Faustina found comfort in the Holy Eucharist. When others demanded more of her than she could physically do, she depended on Jesus' strength, given through the sacrament, to sustain her. When she was too ill to attend Mass, she would make her way there for Communion. When she was too ill for that, others brought Communion to her. During her last, long stay at the sanatorium, when no one could bring her the Host, she received Communion from the hands of an angel.

Faustina returned to the sanatorium in April. She was well cared for, and while there she ministered to others as she was able by listening, prayer, and counsel. By June Sr. Faustina was too ill to write in her diary. During her last weeks she struggled to complete her final notebook. She knew the message of mercy would spread over the whole world.

At the end of August Faustina wrote a letter to Mother Michael, the Mother General. Faustina thanked her for all she had done, for the graces received from the community, and asked forgiveness for any offenses she had committed.

Faustina's condition grew worse. On August 25, her thirty-third birthday, she received the Anointing of the Sick. Fr. Sopocko visited her on August 28 and again on September 2. After taking his leave, he remembered something he had left and returned to her room. He found her in ecstasy and did not disturb her.

On September 17 she was taken home to the convent to die. She lay in a private room, unable to eat. Five days later, according to custom, she formally asked pardon of the entire community. On September 28, Fr. Sopocko made his last visit.

Finally, on October 5, Fr. Andrasz heard her last confession.

For much of the evening she was surrounded by the sisters and the chaplain. After they left, at 10:45 P.M., the one sister who had remained with her ran to summon the others. Sr. Faustina of the Blessed Sacrament looked to heaven and died, united at last with her beloved Jesus.

Her funeral Mass was held on October 7. Not wanting her family to bear the expense and suffering, Faustina had not informed them of her final illness. They were not present at her funeral. After the Mass her coffin was carried to the common grave of the community, and there she was buried. As Faustina herself predicted, her work on earth had just begun.

CHAPTER 2

The Mission of St. Faustina

Although her mission as a professed sister was obedience to her superiors, our Lord also called Faustina to a special mission: She was to be His Apostle of Divine Mercy, proclaiming God's limitless mercy to the world by example and by faithfully recording His revelations. "Glorifying Your mercy," she wrote, "is the exclusive task of my life" (*Diary,* 1242).

Throughout her life she grew in understanding this call. Faustina developed deep humility through obedience to the will of God as expressed through her superiors and her spiritual directors. She conscientiously kept a spiritual diary, as Fr. Sopocko requested. Trusting in God's sustaining grace, she entered fully into the passion of Jesus. Eventually she offered herself completely, her sufferings and her prayers, for the salvation of souls.

Revelations

Faustina was just seven when she first heard Jesus speaking in her soul, and such revelations continued for the rest of her life. Some revelations advised Faustina how to act in particular situations and how to respond to people around her. Others directed her in the journey to oneness with God.

Through them, God guided Faustina as she faced life's major decisions as well as its dull routines. Whether making known His passionate desire for the salvation of souls, or helping her cope with the physical demands of kitchen duty, Jesus was always present to her. The most famous of Faustina's revelations have to do with God's Divine Mercy. The first was of the Image of Divine Mercy, now recognized throughout the world. The revelation that has greatest significance for the whole Church is the Feast of Divine Mercy. Sr. Faustina recorded the desire of the Lord for this Feast at the time of the original revelation of the Image and at fourteen other times:

> **My daughter, tell the whole world about My inconceivable mercy. I desire that the Feast of Mercy be a refuge and shelter for all souls, and especially for poor sinners. On that day the very depths of My tender mercy are open. I pour out a whole ocean of graces upon those souls who approach the fount of My mercy.... Let no soul fear to draw near to Me, even though its sins be as scarlet. My mercy is so great that no mind, be it of man or of angel, will be able to fathom it throughout all eternity. (*Diary*, 699)**

In response to these messages, at the time of his canonization of Faustina, Pope John Paul II proclaimed the first Sunday after Easter as Divine Mercy Sunday for the universal Church.

In another revelation, Jesus taught Faustina a special prayer, the Chaplet of Divine Mercy:

> **This prayer will serve to appease My wrath. You will recite it for nine days, on the beads of the rosary, in the following manner: First of all, you will say one OUR FATHER and HAIL MARY and the I BELIEVE IN GOD. Then on the OUR FATHER beads you will say the following words: "Eternal Father, I offer You the Body and Blood, Soul and Divinity of Your dearly beloved Son, Our Lord Jesus Christ, in atonement for**

our sins and those of the whole world." On the HAIL MARY beads you will say the following words: "For the sake of His sorrowful Passion, have mercy on us and on the whole world." In conclusion, three times you will recite these words: "Holy God, Holy Mighty One, Holy Immortal One, have mercy on us and on the whole world." (*Diary*, 476)

Jesus told Faustina that He would grant the requests of those who recited this prayer. Sinners who prayed it would be filled with peace and would have a happy death.

Write that when they say this chaplet in the presence of the dying, I will stand between My Father and the dying person, not as the just Judge but as the merciful Savior. (*Diary*, 1541)

Preparation for Her Mission

In order to carry out her mission of redemptive suffering for the salvation of sinners and focusing the world's attention on the mercy of God, Faustina gave herself unreservedly to Jesus. She trusted that He would prepare her for her work and sustain her as she strove to remain faithful to His call.

Indeed, Jesus was her Teacher. She wrote:

I would not know how to live without the Lord. Jesus often visits me in this seclusion, teaches me, reassures me, rebukes me, and admonishes me. He himself forms my heart according to His divine wishes and likings, but always with much goodness and mercy. (*Diary*, 1024)

Faustina learned well to respond to His invitation in the Gospel:

"Come to me, all who labor and are burdened, and I will give you rest. Take my yoke upon you and learn from me, for I am meek and humble of heart; and you will find rest for yourselves. For my yoke is easy and my burden light" (Mt 11:28-30).

She was given the ability to see every moment of life as an opportunity to share the Lord's yoke and to deepen her relationship with God. Even routine chores and taunts of other sisters became sources of grace. Jesus encouraged her:

I was your Teacher, I am and I will be; strive to make your heart like unto My humble and gentle Heart. Never claim your rights. Bear with great calm and patience everything that befalls you. Do not defend yourself when you are put to shame, though innocent. Let others triumph. Do not stop being good when you notice that your goodness is being abused. I Myself will speak up for you when it is necessary. (*Diary*, 1701)

Later she would write:

I accept joy or suffering, praise or humiliation with the same disposition. I remember that one and the other are passing. What does it matter to me what people say about me? I have long ago given up everything that concerns my person. My name is host—or sacrifice, not in words but in deeds, in the emptying of myself and in becoming like You on the Cross, O good Jesus, my Master! (*Diary*, 485)

Jesus helped her deal not only with emotional anguish but also with intense physical suffering that plagued Faustina for much of her adult life. Tuberculosis and its complications made completion of assigned chores difficult. Despite tremendous human effort, they sometimes were accomplished only with divine help. Exhaustion and weakness required Faustina to rest, and she spent time in convent infirmaries and in a sanatorium. These periods of rest often invited resentment and cruel remarks from those around her.

Spiritual Trials

Illness was not Faustina's only source of physical suffering. She also experienced agonizing pain from internal stigmata. While this was not constant, it recurred often during her life. As with all afflictions, she willingly embraced it as a means of gaining sanctity. She learned that suffering was God's gift to her:

> Suffering is a great grace; through suffering the soul becomes like the Savior; in suffering love becomes crystallized; the greater the suffering, the purer the love. (*Diary*, 57)

Jesus purified her soul through spiritual trials as well. The dark night that Faustina experienced early in her religious life was one crucible. Only after she had passed through it did she recognize it for what it was:

> After such sufferings the soul finds itself in a state of great purity of spirit and very close to God. But I should add that during these spiritual torments it is close to God, but it is blind. The soul's vision is plunged into darkness, and though God is nearer than ever to the soul which is suffering, the whole secret consists in the fact that it knows

nothing of this. The soul in fact declares that, not only has God abandoned it, but it is the object of His hatred.... Yet despite all, I learned later that God is closer to a soul at such moments than at others, because it would not be able to endure these trials with the help of ordinary grace alone. God's omnipotence and an extraordinary grace must be active here, for otherwise the soul would succumb at the first blow. (*Diary*, 109)

Another spiritual trial was the push and pull of confusion about founding a new congregation. Jesus asked her to do so, but she met resistance at every turn. The matter was a constant source of distress for Faustina. Yet her struggles helped to deepen her complete trust in Jesus.

Nurturing this trust, Jesus sustained Faustina in two other important ways. First, he provided her with a spiritual director, a confessor, and superiors who were sensitive to her unique spiritual journey. Open to God's grace, they all responded to Faustina in ways that helped her along her path to holiness. Jesus admonished her to be obedient to them in all things. Through them He guided His eager pupil along her way, making sure she would not fall into error or be misled.

She wrote of the two priests in her diary:

But my torments are coming to an end. The Lord is giving me the promised help. I can see it in two priests; namely, Father Andrasz and Father Sopocko. During the retreat before my perpetual vows, I was set completely at peace for the first time [by Father Andrasz], and afterwards I was led in the same direction by Father Sopocko. This was the fulfillment of the Lord's promise. (*Diary*, 141)

The other source of strength and nourishment was the sacraments, particularly the Eucharist and Reconciliation. Faustina had a deep love and need for the Eucharist. She grasped its mystery and relied on its power. She makes these revealing statements about her life:

> The most solemn moment of my life is the moment when I receive Holy Communion. I long for each Holy Communion, and for every Holy Communion I give thanks to the Most Holy Trinity. (*Diary*, 1804)

> All the good that is in me is due to Holy Communion. I owe everything to it. (*Diary*, 1392)

The Sacrament of Reconciliation became a regular and important part of Faustina's life. She grew in her understanding of its formative as well as healing effects.

Living Out Her Mission of Mercy

St. Faustina lived her mission of mercy by writing of God's mercy in her diary and by offering everything she did, all her suffering and unceasing prayers, for the salvation of souls. Much of what we know of this comes to us from her diary.

In 1934, during her stay in Vilnius, Sr. Faustina was told by her confessor, Fr. Sopocko, to write down her interior experiences. When asked by someone in the congregation why Sr. Faustina had been writing a diary, Fr. Sopocko answered: "I was a professor at the Seminary and at the School of Theology of the Stefan Batory University in Vilnius at the time. I had no time to listen to her lengthy confessions at the confessional, so

I told her to write everything down and then to show it to me from time to time. This is how the diary came into being" (Fr. Sopocko's letter of March 6, 1972).

In addition to this order from her confessor, Sr. Faustina mentions on many pages of her diary a command to write given her by the Lord Jesus Himself:

January 23, [1937]. I did not feel like writing today. Then I heard a voice in my soul: **My daughter, you do not live for yourself but for souls; write for their benefit.** (*Diary*, 895)

And Jesus said, **Secretary of My most profound mystery, know that yours is an exclusive intimacy with Me. Your task is to write down everything that I make known to you about My mercy, for the benefit of those who by reading these things will be comforted in their souls and will have the courage to approach Me. I therefore want you to devote all your free moments to writing.** (*Diary*, 1693)

Her diary has reached out to the world, not only in the original Polish language but also in English, Spanish, Portuguese, Russian, French, Italian, and German, as well as and through partially translated texts in leaflets in dozens of languages. It is numbered among the outstanding works of mystical literature.

Besides writing, Faustina remained faithful to her call by doing all in her power to bring souls to recognize and accept God's gift of mercy. At times that required her to follow Jesus' spoken commands: She directed the artist as he painted the revealed Image of Divine Mercy. She made known the Chaplet of Divine Mercy, and she encouraged those who were able to work for the establishment of the feast of Divine Mercy.

Beyond this, Faustina offered every aspect of her life to God for the salvation of souls. Jesus told her that she would save more souls through her prayer and sacrifice than missionaries would through their teaching and sermons. He instructed her to embrace all sufferings with love. The Lord demanded works of mercy from Faustina and taught her how to exercise them:

I am giving you three ways of exercising mercy toward your neighbor: the first—by deed, the second—by word, the third—by prayer. In these three degrees is contained the fullness of mercy, and it is an unquestionable proof of love for Me. (*Diary*, 742)

As Faustina strove to live her life as an example of Divine Mercy, she increased her ability to leave her will behind. She abandoned herself to doing the will of God. Her trust in God became absolute. She wrote:

I firmly trust and commit myself entirely to Your holy will, which is mercy itself. (*Diary*, 1574)

From today onward, Your will, Lord, is my food. Lead me, O God, along whatever roads You please; I have placed all my trust in Your will which is, for me, love and mercy itself. (*Diary*, 1264)

Union With God

The Lord grants to certain souls special graces of union with Himself in order to do some great work that is, humanly speaking, absolutely beyond its power.

Know, My daughter, that between Me and you there is a bottomless abyss, an abyss which separates the Creator from the creature. But this abyss is filled with My mercy. I raise you up to Myself, not that I have need of you, but it is solely out of mercy that I grant you the grace of union with Myself. (*Diary,* 1576)

Faustina's union with God empowered her to proclaim God's mercy:

When I entered the chapel, once again the majesty of God overwhelmed me. I felt that I was immersed in God, totally immersed in Him and penetrated by Him, being aware of how much the heavenly Father loves us. Oh, what great happiness fills my heart from knowing God and the divine life! It is my desire to share this happiness with all people. (*Diary,* 491)

In her diary, Faustina attempted to describe her union with God:

My communion with the Lord is now purely spiritual. My soul is touched by God and wholly absorbs itself in Him, even to the complete forgetfulness of self. Permeated by God to its very depths, it drowns in His beauty; it completely dissolves in Him—I am at a loss to describe this, because in writing I am making use of the senses; but there, in that union, the senses are not active; there is a merging of God and the soul; and the life of God to which the soul is admitted is so great that the human tongue cannot express it. (*Diary,* 767)

Union with God included union with the passion of Christ. St. Faustina lived St. Paul's words: "I have been crucified with Christ, and the life I live is not my own" (Gal 2:19-20). Our Lord invited her to the "exclusive privilege" of drinking from the cup which He drank (*Diary*, 1626).

He made it clear to Sister Faustina that she was participating in the great work of salvation:

I am giving you a share in the redemption of mankind. (*Diary*, 310)

Help Me, My daughter, to save souls. Join your sufferings to My passion and offer them to the heavenly Father for sinners. (*Diary*, 1032)

Faustina did join her sufferings with Jesus' passion. On Holy Thursday, 1934, after hearing Him ask her to make an offering of herself for sinners, she made an act of oblation. Later she recorded it in her diary:

Before heaven and earth, before all the choirs of Angels, before the Most Holy Virgin Mary, before all the Powers of heaven, I declare to the One Triune God that today, in union with Jesus Christ, Redeemer of souls, I make a voluntary offering of myself for the conversion of sinners, especially for those souls who have lost hope in God's mercy. This offering consists in my accepting, with total subjection to God's will, all the sufferings, fears and terrors with which sinners are filled. In return, I give them all the consolations which my soul receives from my communion with God. In a word, I offer everything for them: Holy Masses, Holy Communions, penances, mortifications, prayers. (*Diary*, 309)

Later Faustina reflected:

> From this moment on, I live in the deepest peace, because the Lord Himself is carrying me in the hollow of His hand. He, Lord of unfathomable mercy, knows that I desire Him alone in all things, always and everywhere. (*Diary*, 1264)

She learned mercy and humility, and throughout her life found rest by total trust in his merciful heart:

> Christ and Lord, You are leading me over such precipices that, when I look at them, I am filled with fright, but at the same time I am at peace as I nestle close to Your heart. Close to Your Heart, I fear nothing. In these dangerous moments, I act like a little child, carried in its mother's arms; when it sees something which menaces it, it clasps its mother's neck more firmly and feels secure. (*Diary*, 1726)

This deep trust in Jesus enabled her to embrace His will as her own and develop the spirituality that would transform not only her life but also the lives of generations to come.

CHAPTER 3

The Spiritual Life of St. Faustina
Basic Spirituality

The basic spirituality of St. Faustina is the fundamental spirituality of all saints: union with God, built on humble obedience to His will. It is a union of love, received by total abandonment to the Lord. United perfectly with God, the saint becomes a channel for divine love to flow freely to others. His or her life becomes the fulfillment of the great commandments: love God, and love your neighbor.

In over three dozen diary entries, Faustina writes of such union with God. She speaks of how the love of God penetrated her heart and whole being:

At that very moment, I felt some kind of fire in my heart. I feel my senses deadening and have no idea of what is going on around me. I feel the Lord's gaze piercing me through and through. I am very much aware of His greatness and my misery. An extraordinary suffering pervades my soul, together with a joy I cannot compare to anything. I feel powerless in the embrace of God. I feel that I am in Him and that I am dissolved in Him like a drop of water in the ocean. I cannot express what takes place within me; after such interior prayer, I feel strength and power to practice the most difficult virtues. I feel dislike for all things that the world holds in esteem. With all my soul I desire silence and solitude. (*Diary*, 432)

Again she wrote:

> But when I recovered my senses, I felt the strength and
> courage to do God's will; nothing seemed difficult to me;
> and whereas I had previously been making excuses to the
> Lord, I now felt the Lord's courage and strength within
> me, and I said to the Lord, "I am ready for every beck and
> call of Your will!" (*Diary*, 439)

> Already here on earth we can taste the happiness of those
> in heaven by an intimate union with God, a union that is
> extraordinary and often quite incomprehensible to us.
> One can attain this very grace through simple faithfulness
> of soul. (*Diary*, 507)

Devotion to Mary, Mother of God

Faustina had a special devotion to Our Lady, who sometimes
appeared to her and gave her counsel. From Mary, Faustina
deepened her understanding of the importance of the virtues of
humility, purity, and the love of God. Mary cared for Faustina
as a special child, and instructed her to live always in an intimate
union with God.

To Be a Saint

Throughout her life, Faustina desired to attain sainthood. It was
a bold desire to love God as no one has ever loved Him:

> My Jesus, You know that from my earliest years I have
> wanted to become a great saint; that is to say, I have
> wanted to love You with a love so great that there would
> be no soul who has hitherto loved You so. (*Diary*, 1372)

Her resolution to be a saint was "extremely pleasing" to the Lord, and He gave her the conviction that she would attain this destiny. She wanted this sanctity in order to be useful to the Church. She understood that her actions would have a great influence on the whole Church:

> I strive for the greatest perfection possible in order to be useful to the Church. Greater by far is my bond to the Church. The sanctity or the fall of each individual soul has an effect upon the whole Church. (*Diary*, 1475)

Faustina embraced humility, knowing it as the acceptance of our nothingness, or "misery," as she often named it. Humility is the awareness of and response to the fact that *all is gift*. All we are, all we have, all we do, is the gift of God. Her humble response was thanksgiving and praise for His great love and mercy.

She heard the will of God for her life through Scripture, the Church, and her superiors, and through God's word implanted in her heart. She heard and obediently acted upon it.

By canonizing Faustina, the Church officially recognized her humble obedience and her heroic practice of faith, hope, and love. Faustina's lifelong desire was realized.

The Unique Features of the Spirituality of St. Faustina

Though all saints share the basic spirituality of union with God, each also has unique features that distinguish him or her from others. Faustina is a special model of sanctity for our time because of her intense focus on trust in the Divine Mercy. Her life not only makes others aware of the availability of God's limitless mercy, but it also alerts us to the urgent need for that mercy in our day. Therefore, the two main features of her spirituality are trust and mercy.

Trust

Trust is more than faith in God. It includes hope, which is reliance upon Jesus and His promises, as well as love. Pope John Paul II developed the fuller meaning of trust in his encyclical, *Mother of the Redeemer.* He reflected on the main theme of his letter using the words of St. Elizabeth: "Blest is she who trusted (believed) that the Lord's word to her would be fulfilled" (Lk 1:45). "To believe [trust]," he says, "means to 'abandon oneself to the truth of the word of the living God'" (14).

For Faustina, trust was a total abandonment and reliance upon "the truth of the word of the living God."

Examples of trust in the life of St. Faustina are found throughout her diary. Our Lord taught her about the trust He wants of those seeking to be holy:

Let souls who are striving for perfection particularly adore My mercy, because the abundance of graces which I grant them flows from My mercy. I desire that these souls distinguish themselves by boundless trust in My mercy. I Myself will attend to the sanctification of such souls. I will provide them with everything they will need to attain sanctity. The graces of My mercy are drawn by means of one vessel only, and that is—trust. The more a soul trusts, the more it will receive. (*Diary,* 1578)

A diary entry that shows her extreme trust is one made when she renewed her total gift of self to the Lord. He then told her that there was still more to give:

Jesus said to me, **My daughter, you have not offered Me that which is really yours.** I probed deeply into myself and found that I love God with all the faculties of my soul and, unable to see what it was that I had not yet given to the Lord, I asked, "Jesus, tell me what it is, and I will give it to You at once with a generous heart." Jesus said to me with kindness, **Daughter, give Me your misery, because it is your exclusive property.** At that moment, a ray of light illumined my soul, and I saw the whole abyss of my misery. In that same moment I nestled close to the Most Sacred Heart of Jesus with so much trust that even if I had the sins of all the damned weighing on my conscience, I would not have doubted God's mercy but, with a heart crushed to dust, I would have thrown myself into the abyss of Your mercy. I believe, O Jesus, that You would not reject me, but would absolve me through the hand of Your representative. (*Diary*, 1318)

Trust Leads to Thanksgiving

St. Faustina's trust in the mercy of the Lord led her to give thanks to the Father for His great gift of mercy. She gave thanks in suffering:

Jesus, I thank You for the little daily crosses, for opposition to my endeavors, for the hardships of communal life, for the misinterpretation of my intentions, for humiliations at the hands of others, for the harsh way in which we are treated, for false suspicions, for poor health and loss of strength, for self-denial, for dying to myself, for lack of recognition in everything, for the upsetting of all my plans.

Thank You, Jesus, for interior sufferings, for dryness of

spirit, for terrors, fears and incertitudes, for the darkness and the deep interior night, for temptations and various ordeals, for torments too difficult to describe, especially for those which no one will understand, for the hour of death with its fierce struggle and all its bitterness. (*Diary*, 343)

The joy of thanksgiving became a way of life for her:

O my Lord, while calling to mind all Your blessings, in the presence of Your Most Sacred Heart, I have felt the need to be particularly grateful for so many graces and blessings from God. I want to plunge myself in thanksgiving before the Majesty of God ... and although I will outwardly carry out all my duties, my spirit will nonetheless stand continually before the Lord, and all my exercises will be imbued with the spirit of thanksgiving.... I called upon all heaven and earth to join me in my act of thanksgiving. (*Diary*, 1369)

The Divine Mercy

The second unique feature of Faustina's spirituality is her intense focus on Divine Mercy. In his encyclical on Divine Mercy, Pope John Paul II called mercy "the second name of love" and the greatest attribute of God toward mankind. Divine Mercy can be defined in various ways: as God's love poured out in creating, redeeming, and sanctifying us; as love poured out upon sinners; as love of the unlovable and forgiveness of the unforgivable.

Our Lord taught St. Faustina about the mystery of His mercy and His desire that her heart be a channel of His mercy to the world:

My daughter, know that My Heart is mercy itself. From this sea of mercy, graces flow out upon the whole world. No soul that has approached Me has ever gone away unconsoled. All misery gets buried in the depths of My mercy, and every saving and sanctifying grace flows from this fountain. My daughter, I desire that your heart be an abiding place of My mercy. I desire that this mercy flow out upon the whole world through your heart. Let no one who approaches you go away without that trust in My mercy which I so ardently desire for souls. (*Diary*, 1777)

Devotion to the merciful heart of Jesus was central in the spirituality of St. Faustina, as well as in her mission: "O my Jesus, I have only one task to carry out in my lifetime, in death, and throughout eternity, and that is to adore Your incomprehensible mercy" (*Diary*, 1553).

The Gospel Elements of Her Spiritual Life

The basic pattern of the spiritual life of St. Faustina followed the life of Jesus, as did the lives of other mystics and saints. Indeed, we, as disciples of Christ, are all called to model our spiritual lives after the rhythm of Jesus' own. The pattern echoes the trilogy of the paschal mystery: Jesus died, rose by the Spirit, and reigns over the kingdom of God.

In the Gospels, this three-step pattern is seen in the lives of Jesus's disciples: They died to self, rose with their Savior, and with Him, reign over the kingdom. As in Faustina's life, these steps are first purgative, ridding oneself of sin and self-absorption. Next, they are illuminative, leading one to deeper spiritual understanding. Lastly, they are unitive, bringing the soul closer to oneness with God.

Mystics and Saints

Each of the mystics and saints followed this triad approach, but in a unique way. St. John of the Cross progressed from "nada," or nothingness, through "todo," or completeness, to union. His way is sometimes called "the dark way." St. Ignatius of Loyola, following "the discerning way," advanced from desolation, through revelation, and arrived at consolation. The way of St. Faustina can be called "the merciful way." She moved through misery, into mercy, and finally into union with her Lord.

These three elements of spirituality—death by repentance of sin, resurrection through yielding to the Holy Spirit, and residing in the kingdom by abiding in God's love—are repeated as one grows in holiness. They are like waltz steps, and the Lord leads us in ascending spirals as we move through this dance of the Holy Spirit to the house of the Father.

The Merciful Way

Gleaned from her diary, Faustina's merciful way expresses the Gospel elements of death, resurrection, and kingdom. St. Faustina followed "the little way" of St. Thérèse of Lisieux, who put a special focus on littleness and on love. Faustina, who had a great devotion to St. Thérèse (see *Diary,* 150), focused particularly on one's misery and complete trust in God's mercy. She wrote:

> One day during Holy Mass, the Lord gave me a deeper knowledge of His holiness and His majesty, and at the same time I saw my own misery. This knowledge made me happy, and my soul drowned itself completely in His mercy. I felt enormously happy. (*Diary,* 1801)

The Lord told St. Faustina to write about the merciful way for the sake of the miserable:

> **Write this for the benefit of distressed souls: when a soul sees and realizes the gravity of its sins, when the whole abyss of the misery into which it immersed itself is displayed before its eyes, let it not despair, but with trust let it throw itself into the arms of My mercy, as a child into the arms of its beloved mother. These souls have a right of priority to My compassionate Heart, they have first access to My mercy. Tell them that no soul that has called upon My mercy has been disappointed or brought to shame. I delight particularly in a soul which has placed its trust in My goodness.** (*Diary,* 1541)

Divine Mercy Devotions and the Passion of Jesus

Sr. Faustina had a special devotion to the passion. She meditated on it and united her sufferings with those of Jesus, for the salvation of souls. She prayed especially for sinners and the dying, using the mercy devotions the Lord taught her. She prayed unceasingly the Chaplet of The Divine Mercy, as she encouraged others to do.

Veneration of the Image of Divine Mercy was another element of her spirituality. She also would stop at the three o'clock hour and immerse herself in the Passion of Jesus:

> **I remind you, My daughter, that as often as you hear the clock strike the third hour, immerse yourself completely in My mercy, adoring and glorifying it; invoke its omnipotence for the whole world, and particularly for poor sinners; for at that moment mercy was opened wide for every soul. In this hour you can obtain**

everything for yourself and for others for the asking; it was the hour of grace for the whole world—mercy triumphed over justice.

(*Diary*, 1572)

For St. Faustina, the celebration of the Feast of Divine Mercy was the culmination of all the devotions of the Divine Mercy. Like the crucified Jesus, she thirsted for souls. For their salvation, she joined her sufferings to those of her Lord:

Jesus looked at me and said, **Souls perish in spite of My bitter Passion. I am giving them the last hope of salvation; that is, the Feast of My Mercy. If they will not adore My mercy, they will perish for all eternity.** (*Diary*, 965)

After some time, He said, **I thirst. I thirst for the salvation of souls. Help Me, My daughter, to save souls. Join your sufferings to My Passion and offer them to the heavenly Father for sinners.** (*Diary*, 1032)

Faustina summarized her spiritual life as being "drowned" in His mercy, and in her final diary entry encapsulated her spirituality:

And, although I am such misery, I do not fear You, because I know Your mercy well. Nothing will frighten me away from You, O God, because everything is so much less than what I know [Your mercy to be]—I see that clearly. (*Diary*, 1803)

Throughout her life, in her misery, she knew God's mercy and trusted in Him. She lived and died "the merciful way."

CHAPTER 4

Faustina: A Blending of East and West

"Promoting the restoration of unity among all Christians is one of the chief concerns of the Second Sacred Ecumenical Synod of the Vatican." This opening statement of the Second Vatican Council's *Decree on Ecumenism* established the commitment of the Church which Pope John Paul II has carried out as a major thrust of his pontificate. He elaborated on this theme in his encyclical *That They May Be One* (*Ut Unum Sint*). His apostolic letter *The Eastern Light* (*Orientale Lumen*) is an appeal to the Christians of East and West to restore unity.

St. Faustina fulfills the very core of this call to unity. Her life, mission, and spirituality blend elements of both Eastern and Western Church traditions. Her desire for holiness extended to Church unity, especially through her prayers and sacrifices.

The Spark From Poland: Where East and West Meet

St. Faustina Kowalska writes in her diary:

> As I was praying for Poland, I heard the words: **I bear a special love for Poland, and if she will be obedient to My will, I will exalt her in might and holiness. From her will come forth the spark that will prepare the world for My final coming.** (*Diary,* 1732)

This mysterious spark from Poland could been seen as a combination of several people and events: St. Faustina and the message of Divine Mercy, St. Maximilian Kolbe and the role of Mary and the Holy Spirit, Pope John Paul II's consecrating all to Mary, and Lech Walesa and the Solidarity movement, which helped collapse Soviet Communism. These people and their works, individually and together, are sparks that continue to ignite both the East and the West.

The Polish Church is a fascinating combination of Eastern and Western spirituality. Before Poland's official date of conversion in A.D. 966, the missionary apostle St. Cyril and his brother, St. Methodius, brought the Christian faith from Constantinople to Moravia and southeastern Poland.

In *Orientale Lumen*, Pope John Paul II elaborates rich treasures that are integral to the Church of the East. Many of them are evident not only in Polish Catholic spirituality but also in the spirituality of the Divine Mercy as revealed to and lived out by St. Faustina. In *Orientale Lumen*, Pope John Paul II exhorts us to implore the Divine Mercy for unity of the Churches of the East and West.

St. Faustina Kowalska is the apostle of Divine Mercy in our time, and her message, exemplified by her life, is the spark that will enkindle the unity of the Churches of the East and West that is to prepare for the final coming of the Lord. She lived an amazing blend of Eastern and Western spirituality. Her life helps unlock the mysteries of both.

Icons and Other Devotions

A variety of Eastern elements have become part of Polish Catholic devotional life over the centuries and were woven into the life of St. Faustina. The Eastern tradition of icons is one example. In his book *Behold the Beauty of the Lord: Praying with Icons* (page 13), Henri Nouwen says that the "Byzantine fathers focus on gazing."[1] Icons are painted for the purpose of helping the one who gazes at them to enter into an experience of prayer. Icons may appear flat and stylized to one more accustomed to Western religious art. However, as Henri Nouwen explains, "They do not reveal themselves to us at first sight. It is only gradually, after a patient, prayerful presence that they start speaking to us. And as they speak, they speak more to our inner than to our outer senses. They speak to the heart that searches for God."[2]

In Poland the appreciation of icons is seen in the veneration of the icon of Our Lady of Czestochowa and many others in parish churches and shrines throughout the country. Most homes have a prayer corner honoring the household icon. Faustina herself obtained permission to visit the icon of Our Lady of Czestochowa, where she spent hours in prayer before the image.

The blessing of food baskets at Easter and the sharing of the bread wafer (oplatek) at the vigil of Christmas are other Polish customs. Sharing the wafer was a significant moment in the devotion of St. Faustina at the vigil of Christmas (*Diary*, 436, 524, 845, 1438).

Common hymns such as the Thrice-Holy Hymn and those by St. Ephraim, the Good Friday Lamentations, the burial service of Our Lord, and the Easter Sunday Mass at dawn are other traditional practices of Polish Catholics.

[1]Henri J.M. Nouwen, *Behold the Beauty of the Lord*. (Notre Dame, Ind.: Ave Maria, 1987), 13.
[2]Nouwen, 13.

Treasures of the Christian East
in the Life of St. Faustina

Sacred Liturgy and Eucharist

Using the rich experiences of faith in the Eastern Church enumerated in *Orientale Lumen,* one is able to see how Faustina integrated treasures of the East into her spiritual life. One treasure is devotion to the sacred liturgy, especially the Eucharist. The key to the life of Sr. Maria Faustina of the Blessed Sacrament was the Holy Eucharist. Almost every page of her diary makes a reference to it.

There are a number of "special" aspects of her relationship to the Holy Eucharist, among them her profound understanding of the mystery of this gift of God. She describes it as the greatest gift of His presence.

Participation in Divine Life Through the Holy Trinity

The goal of Christian life, as seen from the perspective of the East, is participation in God's life through communion with the mystery of the Trinity. St. Faustina prayed for transformation into the living image and likeness of God, being drawn into the Holy Trinity:

> My Jesus, penetrate me through and through so that I might be able to reflect You in my whole life. Divinize me so that my deeds have supernatural value. (*Diary,* 1242)

She also attempts to describe her *experience* of divinization:

> I saw the joy of the Incarnate Word, and I was immersed in the Divine Trinity. When I came to myself, longing filled my soul, and I yearned to be united with God. (*Diary,* 1121)

Divinization in the Sacraments Through the Holy Spirit

The reality of divinization, or the understanding of St. Irenaeus' assertion that "God passed into man so that man might pass into God" ("Against Heresies"), is part of the heritage of the Eastern churches. In the diary of St. Faustina we read about her desire to become transformed into a "living Host":

Jesus, transform me, miserable and sinful as I am, into Your own self (for You can do all things), and give me to Your Eternal Father. I want to be a *sacrificial host* before You, but an ordinary wafer to people. I want the fragrance of my sacrifice to be known to You alone. (*Diary,* 483)

The experience of being a living host—hidden, broken, and given—was the central experience of her life. She knew it most profoundly in conjunction with the Holy Eucharist, either during Mass and Holy Communion or during adoration of the Blessed Sacrament.

The Virgin Mary, Mother of God and Icon of the Church

Mary holds a special place in the Eastern Church. St. Faustina honored the Mother of God in a unique way. On the day of her perpetual vows Faustina addressed Mary and prayed:

Mother of God, Most Holy Mary, my Mother, you are my mother in a *special* way because your beloved Son is my Bridegroom, and thus we are both your children. For your Son's sake, you have to love me. O Mary, my dearest Mother, guide my spiritual life in such a way that it will please your Son. (*Diary,* 240)

This prayer was answered in an extraordinary way when Mary appeared to her and said:

> *My daughter, at God's command I am to be, in a special and exclusive way your Mother; but I desire that you, too, in a special way be my child.* (*Diary,* 1414)

On the Feast of the Annunciation, March 25, 1936, Mary appeared to Sr. Faustina explaining her mission: "Speak to the world about His great mercy and prepare for His second coming." Mary's role was to prepare Faustina by being a Mother to her, guiding and teaching her about the life of union with God, and strengthening her in sufferings by suffering along with her (*Diary,* 25, 309, 316, 635).

Sr. Faustina prayed to the Mother of God for this mission throughout her life. She regularly celebrated the feasts of Mary with special anticipation and joy. The rosary of Our Lady was part of her prayer.

Faustina reflected that "the more I imitate the Mother of God, the more deeply I get to know God" (*Diary,* 843). For Faustina, Mary was truly her mother, and she could nestle close to her Immaculate Heart like a child. (*Diary,* 1097).

The Trinity: Unknowable, Divine.

In *Orientale Lumen,* Pope John Paul II notes the deep sense of mystery in Eastern churches. He reiterates their sense of God's essence being unknowable. We can only know that God *is.* From her experience, St. Faustina wrote many entries on the mystery of the Holy Trinity. This is one example:

> On one occasion I was reflecting on the Holy Trinity, on the essence of God. I absolutely wanted to know and fathom

who God is.... In an instant my spirit was caught up into what seemed to be the next world. I saw an inaccessible light, and in this light what appeared like three sources of light which I could not understand. And out of that light came words in the form of lightning which encircled heaven and earth. Not understanding anything, I was very sad. Suddenly, from this sea of inaccessible light came our dearly beloved Savior, unutterably beautiful with His shining wounds. And from this light came a voice which said, **Who God is in His Essence, no one will fathom, neither the mind of Angels nor of man.** Jesus said to me, **Get to know God by contemplating His attributes.** A moment later, He traced the sign of the cross with His hand and vanished. (*Diary*, 30)

Other Elements of Eastern Spirituality Stressed by John Paul II in *Orientale Lumen*

Gospel, Churches, and Culture

When Sts. Cyril and Methodius brought their faith to new places, they were careful to adopt the customs and language of those with whom they lived. Respect for cultural differences, and taking them into account when evangelizing, is another aspect of the Eastern Church that is echoed in the life of St. Faustina.

As requested by Our Lord, she wrote everything the Lord taught her about Divine Mercy. Faustina wrote simply and clearly in her native Polish. She had only two winters of schooling, and so it is amazing that her writing is so transparent and understandable. Her great love of the Lord and His Church shines through her writing. Because of Faustina's special knowledge of the Divine Mercy, the reader easily comes to understand and share in her mission of proclaiming the Divine Mercy. She lived and witnessed the heart of the Gospel to ordinary people.

Between Memory and Expectation
The rich tradition of the Church passes on the history and truths of Jesus' life to every generation of believers. Tradition gives us continuity with the past. The Eastern Church is particularly able to balance a sense of connectedness to the past while being open to God's future.

St. Faustina was deeply rooted in the tradition of the Gospel and the Church. She shared in the life of Jesus from infancy to the cross. While she lived a life of childlike simplicity, in imitation of the child Jesus, she also repeatedly shared in His passion.

Faustina's mission was also one of expectation. She lived it out to prepare for the coming of the Lord. Our Lady spoke to St. Faustina about the urgency of mercy:

> *I gave the Savior to the world; as for you, you have to speak to the world about His great mercy and prepare the world for the Second Coming of Him who will come, not as a merciful Savior, but as a just Judge. (Diary, 635)*

Faustina lived in the present with her roots sunk deeply into the past. She opened herself to prepare for and receive whatever God's future would bring.

Monasticism, a Bridge Between East and West
Monastic life had its beginnings in the deserts of the East. There it was seen as an expression of everyone's baptismal call. Pope John Paul II named it the "very soul of the Eastern Churches" (*Orientale Lumen*). Later, monasticism was passed on to the

West, where it developed a variety of expressions. Since the monastic life is lived by monks and sisters in both East and West, it stands as a concrete expression of the unity desired by Christ.

St. Faustina lived the monastic life to perfection. She experienced her religious vows as a means by which God united Himself to her. She expressed her attitude toward the rule of religious life with simplicity:

> I asked the Lord to grant me the grace that my nature be immune and resist the influences that sometimes try to draw me away from the spirit of our rule and from the minor regulations. These minor transgressions are like little moths that try to destroy (the spiritual life within us and they surely will destroy) it if the soul is aware of these minor transgressions and yet disregards them as small things. I can see nothing that is small in the religious life. (*Diary*, 306)

Reflecting monasticism's relevance to all the faithful, Faustina described a new congregation that would be open to all the baptized as a model of the Christian life. Under the direction of the Lord she described three levels of community, like concentric circles: The inner circle of cloistered contemplatives begging for mercy for the world; the middle circle of active contemplatives; and the outer circle of dedicated laity doing works of mercy.

Between Word and Eucharist
One facet of monasticism shared by East and West is the ideal of living both in personal response to the Word of God and in communal celebration of the Eucharist. The latter is the culmination of prayer life, which plunges the monastic into relationship with the ecclesial community.

St. Faustina's life was truly suspended between the two poles: the Word of God and the Eucharist. She lived the Word of God, especially the Beatitudes. Toward the end of her life Jesus Himself directed her meditation of the Gospel according to St. John:

> **Today, My daughter, for your reading you shall take chapter nineteen of St. John's Gospel, and read it, not only with your lips, but with your heart.** (*Diary,* 1765)

The culmination of her prayer life was the Eucharist.

Liturgy for the Whole Man, the Whole Cosmos

As Pope John Paul II says in *Orientale Lumen,* the liturgy of the Eastern Church strives to involve the entire person in its celebration. All are called, body and soul, to praise and to beauty. Along with humanity, all creation is gathered into the Eucharist of the Lord.

The Liturgy of the Eucharist was central to the life of St. Faustina. Holy Communion was a "common-union-in-Christ," a union with Christ and all members of the church in heaven and earth. Through this union with Christ, Faustina implored mercy on the world.

The special place of the Holy Eucharist in her life can be summed up in her official name, Sr. Maria Faustina of the Most Blessed Sacrament, and in the name she called herself: "My name is to be 'sacrifice'" (*Diary,* 135). Her greatest desire was to be Eucharist: hidden like Jesus, blessed by her union with the Lord, broken like Jesus in the Passion, and totally given for the salvation of souls.

A Clear Look at Self-Discovery

To those desiring true self-discovery, the East offers the school of contemplative gazing upon Christ. The more one trains the inner eye to look in this way, the more one becomes like Christ. Every moment becomes a moment of conversion. Eventually one is able to recognize one's own sin and let go of what keeps one from being filled with God's Spirit.

Every page of Faustina's diary is a record of her intimate union with Christ. Her whole being was turned to him in constant conversation. Aware of her misery and nothingness, she plunged into the Divine Mercy with utter trust:

> You know, Lord, how weak I am. I am an abyss of wretchedness, I am nothingness itself.... However, beyond all abandonment I trust, and in spite of my own feeling I trust, and I am being completely transformed into trust— often in spite of what I feel. (*Diary,* 1489)

With great devotion, Faustina did come to the merciful heart of Jesus in a profound union of hearts, and she found the rest of peace. She took His cross as a victim of love for the sake of others. She learned mercy and humility from Jesus who formed her after the model of His own heart.

A Father in the Spirit

In both Eastern and Western monasticism, individuals are often given a spiritual director. These guides share their Spirit-given gift of helping each person in their care to discern his or her path to God.

Our world desperately needs such spiritual guides. St. Faustina was aware of the need of a spiritual guide. She pleaded with the Lord until she received a special spiritual father in the person of Fr. Michael Sopocko.

Oh, if only I had had a spiritual director from the beginning, then I would not have wasted so many of God's graces.... Oh, how careful confessors should be about the work of God's grace in their penitents' souls! This is a matter of great importance. By the graces given to a soul, one can recognize the degree of its intimacy with God. (*Diary*, 35)

By her example and the wisdom recorded in her diary, Faustina herself has become a much needed spiritual guide for our times.

Communion and Service

As a monk becomes more detached from things that draw him away from God and grows in communion with the Lord, his prayer is more identified with the prayer of Christ. He shares in God's love for humanity and creation. In prayer he invokes the Holy Spirit on the world. Such communion leads to the desire to serve others. Evangelization in its many forms is an important expression of service born of such a relationship with God.

St. Faustina was in close communion with the Lord, and it was because of this union that her great mission of service was so powerful. In the diary text selected for the Liturgy of the Hours for her feast on October 5, she describes her mission of pleading for mercy in order that souls come to know God.

O my God, I am conscious of my mission in the Holy Church. It is my constant endeavor to plead for mercy for the world. I unite myself closely with Jesus and stand before Him as an atoning sacrifice on behalf of the world. God will refuse me nothing when I entreat Him with the voice of His Son. My sacrifice is nothing in itself, but when I join it to the sacrifice of Jesus Christ, it becomes all-powerful and has the power to appease divine wrath. (*Diary*, 482)

74

Relationship With God

Union with God is a great mystery! How can a mere creature be united in an intimate way with Almighty God? It is a mystery of mercy. It is all a gift of love and can only be explained by love alone. God our creator is in love with us. Our perfection is our union with God. Molded in the image of the Son by the Holy Spirit, the monk strives to become the "icon of the Icon."

The texts of the diary of St. Faustina on union with God reveal an extraordinary call to her by Christ to an intimate spiritual union with Him. The purpose of this gift of union is to enable Faustina to do a great work and to resonate with kindred souls for guidance.

In a simple, humble way, she describes the characteristics of union with God. It is an intimate, close, and continuous presence of God that penetrates and permeates her whole being. What a "mystery of mercy" that our God should delight to dwell in the hearts of His creatures!

Silence: The Language of God

The wisdom of the Eastern tradition teaches that the more one increases in knowledge of God, the more one realizes that God is unknowable. Only through what Pope John Paul II calls "adoring silence" (*Orientale Lumen*, #16) does one grow closer to experiencing God's presence. St. Faustina learned this mysterious language of God, silence:

> The Holy Spirit does not speak to a soul that is distracted and garrulous. He speaks by His quiet inspirations to a soul that is recollected, to a soul that knows how to keep silence. (*Diary*, 552)

We all need the silent adoration of the living God. Before His mystery of mercy we have no words adequate to express our response. How we need the witness of St. Faustina in our time of chaotic flood of words, words, words. Our hearts need to explode with a burst of adoration of the mystery of God's mercy, present in our hearts. We need to live in silent spiritual communion with Love poured into our hearts by the gift of the Holy Spirit.

The Treasures of Western Christianity in the Life of St. Faustina

Eucharist, Holy Mary, Peter

St. Faustina also lived the three treasures of the West in the way that they had developed over the centuries: the Eucharist, Mary, and Peter. The Holy Eucharist is the summit of mediated graces in the sacraments. Mary is the Queen of mediated intercession. Peter is the Vicar of Christ, the "prime minister" of mediated authority.

Mediation was a real issue of difference between Catholicism and Reformation Protestantism, which focused so strongly on the divinity of the Lord that it neglected the full appreciation of His humanity. The Catholic response was to focus on the incarnate Word, who truly became flesh and used creation to mediate His grace, intercession, and authority.

In the life of St. Faustina we find her dedication and devotion to the Holy Eucharist expressed in both the celebration of Holy Mass and adoration of the reserved Blessed Sacrament. When she was in her final sickness, an angel came to bring her Holy Communion. She spent every free moment in adoration of the Blessed Sacrament.

Faustina's devotion to the Mother of God expressed itself in her recognition of her greatness by honoring her in her various titles. Faustina often made novenas in preparation for Mary's great feasts: the Immaculate Conception, the Assumption, Our Lady of Czestochowa, and Mother of Mercy. Above all, Faustina's devotion was to be a special daughter and imitate Mary's virtues.

Faustina's respect and obedience to authority, including her religious superiors, was exceptional. In all matters she deferred to her confessor, spiritual director, bishop, and the Holy Father. She regularly prayed for those in authority.

Classic Atonement

Besides the three Catholic treasures of the Eucharist, Mary, and Peter, St. Faustina lived and proclaimed a balanced classic atonement. She knew that Christ redeemed us by His death and resurrection. She also recognized that we must cooperate with His grace by trust in Him, receive His mercy, and share it with our neighbor.

This message of a balanced and classic atonement means that we cannot merit our justification or the forgiveness of our sins, but we do merit our growth in holiness and our eternal life. (See the *Catechism of the Catholic Church,* #2006 to 2011.) We draw upon the atonement of Jesus Christ for the forgiveness of our sins and those of the whole world (see 1 Jn 2:2, NIV).

Faustina is a model of holiness and of evangelization. She is a witness of a life of mercy, bringing together the various treasures of both Eastern and Western spirituality. She is the model of Church unity that can be. She is the "spiritual guide" that we so need in our time. She herself *is* the message of Divine Mercy. She became the "icon of the Icon," a transforming presence of Jesus Christ, Mercy Incarnate.

Chapter 5

Faustina: Saint for the Third Millennium

Spread of the Divine Mercy Devotions

Two years after the death of Faustina, the devotion to the Divine Mercy began spreading in Vilnius. The sisters of her own order, having used a booklet of prayers for this devotion assembled by Fr. Sopocko, did not know that Sr. Faustina was the author. In 1941, Mother Michael Moraczewska informed them of Faustina's mission.

Soon the devotion spread across Poland. It was carried to other countries by soldiers who became acquainted with it during World War II. Nevertheless, on March 6, 1959, after considering some incomplete and inaccurate accounts of Faustina's visions and mission, the Holy See prohibited further spread of the devotion. Most sites where the devotion had been observed responded to the "Notification" by discontinuing the prayers and veneration of the Divine Mercy Image. However, the convent of the Sisters of Our Lady of Mercy in Lagiewniki, with the permission of their archbishop, continued their devotions and their display of the Divine Mercy Image.

St. Faustina and Pope John Paul II

The influence of St. Faustina on Pope John Paul II began in the early 1940s when he was in the clandestine seminary in Krakow. His classmate, now Andrew Cardinal Deskur, told him about the mystic Sr. Faustina Kowalska and the message of Divine Mercy that she had received from the Lord. During that time

Karol Wojtyla worked in the Solvay plant, which could be seen from the convent cemetery where Faustina was buried.

During his years in Krakow, first as a priest and then as a bishop, he made use of the convent as a place of retreat and gave retreats there as well. During the Second Vatican Council, Archbishop Karol Wojtyla conferred with Cardinal Ottaviani about the desire of the faithful in Poland to have Sr. Faustina raised to the honors of the altar. Cardinal Ottaviani told him to gather the sworn testimonies of those who knew her, while they were still alive.

Archbishop Karol Wojtyla delegated his auxiliary bishop, Julian Groblicki, to begin the Informative Process of the life and virtues of Sr. Faustina. In September 1967 the process was completed, and in January 1968, the Process of Beatification was inaugurated.

Because of the positive outcome of the Informative Process, inquiries from many places, especially from Poland and, in particular, from Archbishop Cardinal Wojtyla, were sent to the Sacred Congregation for the Doctrine of the Faith. They asked whether the prohibitions of the 1959 "Notification" were still in effect. In response to these inquiries, the Sacred Congregation issued a new "Notification" dated April 15, 1978, which stated:

This Sacred Congregation, having now in possession the many original documents, unknown in 1959; having taken into consideration the profoundly changed circumstances, and having taken into account the opinion of many Polish Ordinaries, declares no longer binding the prohibitions contained in the quoted "Notification" (of 1959).

Dives in Misericordia

On the first Sunday of Advent, November 30, 1980, Pope John Paul II published his second encyclical letter *Rich in Mercy* (*Dives in Misericordia*), in which he describes the mercy of God as the presence of love which is greater than evil, greater than sin, and greater than death. In it he summons the Church to plead for God's mercy on the whole world.

The publishing of his second encyclical was a significant event in the life of the Holy Father and in his relationship to Faustina and the Divine Mercy message and devotion. George Weigel, in *Witness to Hope: The Biography of Pope John Paul II* (Harper-Collins, 1999), records his personal interview with John Paul II about the encyclical on Divine Mercy and the influence of Faustina:

> As Archbishop of Krakow, Wojtyla had defended Sr. Faustina when her orthodoxy was being posthumously questioned in Rome, due in large part to a faulty translation into Italian of her diary, and had promoted the cause of her beatification. John Paul II, who said that he felt spiritually "very near" to Sr. Faustina, had been "thinking about her for a long time" when he began *Dives in Misericordia*. (Author's personal conversation with Pope John Paul II, January 16, 1997, p. 387.)

This quote expresses the pope's personal witness to the influence of Faustina and the Divine Mercy message and devotion on his life. There are more of these influences in his life, to which he personally testifies.

On November 22, 1981, Pope John Paul II made his first public visit outside of Rome following a lengthy recuperation. On the Feast of Christ the King, he traveled to the Shrine of

Merciful Love in Collevalenza, near Todi, Italy. There, within a few days, an international congress was held to reflect on the Encyclical *Dives in Misericordia*.

After celebrating the Holy Sacrifice of the Eucharist, he made a strong public declaration about the importance of the message of mercy:

> A year ago I published the encyclical *Dives in Misericordia*. This circumstance made me come to the Sanctuary of Merciful Love today. By my presence I wish to reconfirm, in a way, the message of that encyclical. I wish to read it again and deliver it again.
>
> Right from the beginning of my ministry in St. Peter's See in Rome, I considered this message my special task. Providence has assigned it to me in the present situation of man, the Church, and the world. It could be said that precisely this situation assigned that message to me as my task before God. (John Paul II at The Shrine of Merciful Love in Collevalenga, Italy, November 22, 1981)

Blessed Faustina

On Mercy Sunday, April 10, 1991, two years prior to the beatification of Sr. Faustina, John Paul II spoke about Sr. Faustina, relating her to his encyclical and emphasizing her role in bringing the message of mercy to the world:

> The words of the encyclical on Divine Mercy (*Dives in Misericordia*) are particularly close to us. They recall the figure of the Servant of God, Sr. Faustina Kowalska. This simple woman religious particularly brought the Easter message of the merciful Christ closer to Poland and the whole world....

On Mercy Sunday, April 18, 1993, Sr. Faustina was beatified by Pope John Paul II in St. Peter's Square. He began his homily with a quotation from her diary:

> *"I clearly feel that my mission does not end with death, but begins,"* Sr. Faustina wrote in her diary. And it truly did! Her mission continues and is yielding astonishing fruit. It is truly marvelous how her devotion to the merciful Jesus is spreading in our contemporary world and gaining so many human hearts! This is doubtlessly a sign of the times—a sign of our twentieth century. The balance of this century which is now ending, in addition to the advances which have often surpassed those of preceding eras, presents a deep restlessness and fear of the future. Where, if not in the Divine Mercy, can the world find refuge and the light of hope? Believers understand that perfectly.

Mercy: Hope for the World

"Where, if not in the Divine Mercy, can the world find refuge and the light of hope?" is an expression of the theme of John Paul II's pontificate.

In his "Regina Caeli" talk of April 23, 1995, immediately after he had concluded celebrating Divine Mercy Sunday at Holy Spirit Church, John Paul II exhorted us to personally experience God's mercy:

> In a special way, today is the Sunday of thanksgiving for the goodness God has shown man in the whole Easter mystery. This is why it is also called the *Sunday of Divine Mercy*. Essentially, God's mercy, as the mystical experience of Blessed Faustina Kowalska, who was raised to the honors of the altar two years ago, helps us to understand, reveals

precisely this truth: good triumphs over evil, life is stronger than death and God's love is more powerful than sin. All this is manifested in Christ's paschal mystery, in which God appears to us as he is: a tender-hearted *Father*, who does not give up in the face of his children's ingratitude and is always ready to forgive.

Dear brothers and sisters, we must personally experience this mercy if, in turn, we want to be capable of mercy. *Let us learn to forgive!* The spiral of hatred and violence which stains with blood the path of so many individuals and nations can only be broken by the *miracle of forgiveness*.

When Pope John Paul II made a pilgrimage to the Shrine of Divine Mercy in Lagiewniki, Poland, on June 7, 1997, he addressed the Sisters of the Congregation of Our Lady of Mercy in a very personal way, reflecting on Divine Mercy and giving an amazing personal witness to the influence of Sr. Faustina and her message:

I have come here to this shrine as a pilgrim to take part in the unending hymn in honor of Divine Mercy. The psalmist of the Lord had intoned it, expressing what every generation preserved and will continue to preserve as a most precious fruit of faith.

There is nothing that man needs more than Divine Mercy—that love which is benevolent, which is compassionate, which raises man above his weakness to the infinite heights of the holiness of God.

In this place we become particularly aware of this. From here, in fact, went out the Message of Divine Mercy that Christ himself chose to pass on to our generation through Blessed Faustina.

And it is a *message that is clear and understandable for everyone*. Anyone can come here, look at this image of the merciful Jesus, His Heart radiating grace, and hear in the depths of his own soul what Blessed Faustina heard: *"Fear nothing; I am with you always"* (*Diary*, 586).

And if this person responds with a sincere heart: *"Jesus, I trust in you,"* he will find comfort in all his *anxieties and fears....* The message of Divine Mercy has always been near and dear to me. It is as if history had inscribed it in the tragic experience of the Second World War. In those difficult years it was a particular support and an inexhaustible source of hope, not only for the people of Kraków but for the entire nation.

This was also my personal experience, which I took with me to the See of Peter and which in a sense forms the image of this Pontificate....

Do not neglect any of these dimensions of the apostolate. Fulfil it in union with the Archbishop of Kraków, to whose heart is so dear the devotion to the Divine Mercy, and it in union with the whole ecclesial community over which he presides.

The Twofold Canonization of St. Faustina

On Mercy Sunday, April 30, 2000, before some two hundred fifty thousand pilgrims and the television cameras of the world, Pope John Paul II canonized Sr. Faustina Kowalska, "the great apostle of Divine Mercy." In doing so, he also "canonized" the Divine Mercy message and devotion by declaring the Second Sunday of Easter as "Divine Mercy Sunday" for the universal Church.

In one of the most extraordinary homilies of his pontificate, Pope John Paul II repeated three times that Sr. Faustina is

"God's gift to our time." She made the message of Divine Mercy the "bridge to the third millennium." He then said:

> By this act of canonization of Sr. Faustina I intend today to pass this message on to the third millennium. I pass it on to all people, so that they will learn to know ever better the true face of God and the true face of their neighbor. In fact, love of God and love of one's neighbor are inseparable.

Exhorting all of us to join our voices to Mary, Mother of Mercy, and St. Faustina, "who made her life a hymn to mercy" and directing us to "sing the mercies of the Lord for ever" (Ps 89:2), he ended the homily with these words:

> And you, Faustina, a gift of God to our time, a gift from the land of Poland to the whole Church, obtain for us an awareness of the depth of Divine Mercy; help us to have a living experience of it and to bear witness to it among our brothers and sisters. May your message of light and hope spread throughout the world, spurring sinners to conversion, calming rivalries and hatred, and opening individuals and nations to the practice of brotherhood.
>
> Today, fixing our gaze with you on the face of the risen Christ, let us make our own your prayer of trusting abandonment and say with firm hope: Christ Jesus, I trust in you! Jezu, ufam tobie!

Our Response

Universal holiness is the strong and clear mandate given in the Dogmatic Constitution on the Church, one of the main documents of the Vatican Council. We have seen in Faustina's great desire to be a saint the fulfillment of this mandate. By canonizing her, the Church has established her as a model of sanctity for all. Following the example of St. Faustina as Pope John Paul II encourages us to do, we find many ways to grow to be an apostle of Divine Mercy.

Trust in Jesus and Desire for Sainthood

The central message of St. Faustina's life is complete trust in Jesus. Her great trust enabled her to attain her goal of sainthood. In her diary she teaches us that the desire for holiness combined with complete trust in God's mercy make sainthood accessible to all:

> O my Jesus, how very easy it is to become holy; all that is needed is a bit of good will. If Jesus sees this little bit of good will in the soul, He hurries to give himself to the soul, and nothing can stop Him, neither shortcomings nor falls—absolutely nothing. Jesus is anxious to help that soul, and if it is faithful to this grace from God, it can very soon attain the highest holiness possible for a creature here on earth. God is very generous and does not deny His grace to anyone. Indeed He gives more than what we ask of Him. Faithfulness to the inspirations of the Holy Spirit—that is the shortest route. (*Diary*, 291)

Jesus tells us that He will do it if only we trust in Him:

> **My dearest secretary, write that I want to pour out My divine life into human souls and to sanctify them, if only they were willing to accept My grace. The greatest sinners would achieve great sanctity, if only they would trust in My mercy.** (*Diary*, 1784)

Prayer

Faustina's entire life was given to prayer. She prayed with words and in silent contemplation, keeping herself always mindful of God's indwelling presence. Such a constant attitude of prayer is possible to attain, even in the busy world.

Of course, all are encouraged to pray the prayers of devotion to the Divine Mercy. Faustina encourages all to ask for the Holy Spirit to fill them and set them on fire with the love of God. She instructs the faithful to ask for God's mercy in order to forgive and to remove the obstacles to unity. Such forgiveness makes possible the unity that Jesus desires.

Prayer also takes the form of praise and thanksgiving. By giving thanks always and everywhere, we acknowledge that God is God, that He knows and loves us, and cares for us in every circumstance of our lives.

St. Faustina's prayer included reverent reception of the sacraments and daily attendance at Mass. These elements of her spirituality can inspire us to increase our own participation in the sacramental life of the Church.

Perseverance

Whether the anguish was physical or spiritual, Faustina embraced suffering with the spirit of Jesus. Everything that the merciful God has arranged for us to experience at every moment is the best and holiest thing possible. Therefore, we should rejoice and give thanks, with an active abandonment to God's will, not just a passive submission, and then do the best we can in each and every vicissitude. As we do this, we can entrust all our concerns to the merciful heart of Jesus and to the heart of Mary, Mother of Mercy.

Evangelization

We can evangelize in many ways. One means is telling others what God's mercy has done in our lives. We can tell them to snuggle close to the merciful heart of Jesus (*Diary*, 1074).

As St. Augustine said, we should evangelize by the witness of our lives, using words only if we have to. Faustina instructs us to evangelize by living lives of mercy toward others. Her vision of a new congregation included a circle of members that could include everyone in the world. No vows would be required of this group. Prayer and deeds of mercy would be their duties:

> A member of this group ought to perform at least one act of mercy a day; at least one, but there can be many more, for such deeds can easily be carried out by anyone, even the very poorest. For there are three ways of performing an act of mercy: the merciful word, by forgiving and by comforting; secondly, if you can offer no word, then pray—that too is mercy; and thirdly, deeds of mercy. And when the Last Day comes, we shall be judged from this, and on this basis we shall receive the eternal verdict. (*Diary*, 1158)

Summary

Faustina's life directs us to ask for the Lord's mercy and pray for the Holy Spirit to rest on all so we may be one. She tells us to be merciful to everyone, everywhere and at all times, even as our Father is merciful. We are to completely trust in Jesus—trust with a living faith, a lively hope, and a life-giving love. As we strive to live the merciful way, we make Faustina's prayer our own: Jesus, I trust in You.

CHAPTER 6

Prayers and Diary Excerpts
Chaplet of the Divine Mercy

You will recite it for nine days, on the beads of the rosary, in the following manner: First of all, you will say one **OUR FATHER and HAIL MARY and the I BELIEVE IN GOD.** Then on the OUR FATHER beads you will say the following words: "Eternal Father, I offer You the Body and Blood, Soul and Divinity of Your dearly beloved Son, Our Lord Jesus Christ, in atonement for our sins and those of the whole world." On the HAIL MARY beads you will say the following words: "For the sake of His sorrowful Passion have mercy on us and on the whole world." In conclusion, three times you will recite these words: "Holy God, Holy Mighty One, Holy Immortal One, have mercy on us and on the whole world." (*Diary,* 476)

Prayer of Daily Renewal:

O Blood and Water which gushed forth from the Heart of Jesus as a Fount of Mercy for us, I trust in You! (*Diary,* 309)

On Daily Routine:

O life so dull and monotonous, how many treasures you contain! When I look at everything with the eyes of faith, no two hours are alike, and the dullness and monotony disappear. The grace which is given me in this hour will not be repeated in the next. It may be given me again, but it will not be the same grace. (*Diary,* 62)

For Divinization:

My Jesus, penetrate me through and through so that I might be able to reflect You in my whole life. Divinize me so that my deeds may have supernatural value. Grant that I may have love, compassion, and mercy for every soul without exception. (*Diary*, 1242)

A Prayer to Be Merciful:

O Most Holy Trinity! As many times as I breathe, as many times as my heart beats, as many times as my blood pulsates through my body, so many thousand times do I want to glorify Your mercy.

I want to be completely transformed into Your mercy and to be Your living reflection, O Lord. May the greatest of all divine attributes, that of Your unfathomable mercy, pass through my heart and soul to my neighbor.

Help me, O Lord, that my eyes may be merciful, so that I may never suspect or judge from appearances, but look for what is beautiful in my neighbors' souls and come to their rescue.

Help me, that my ears may be merciful, so that I may give heed to my neighbors' needs and not be indifferent to their pains and moanings.

Help me, O Lord, that my tongue may be merciful, so that I should never speak negatively of my neighbor, but have a word of comfort and forgiveness for all.

Help me, O Lord, that my hands may be merciful and filled with good deeds, so that I may do only good to my neighbors and take upon myself the more difficult and toilsome tasks.

Help me, that my feet may be merciful, so that I may hurry to assist my neighbor, overcoming my own fatigue and weariness. My true rest is in the service of my neighbor.

Help me, O Lord, that my heart may be merciful so that I myself may feel all the sufferings of my neighbor. I will refuse my heart to no one. I will be sincere even with those who, I know, will abuse my kindness. And I will lock myself up in the most merciful Heart of Jesus. I will bear my own suffering in silence. May Your mercy, O Lord, rest upon me.

You Yourself command me to exercise the three degrees of mercy. The first: the act of mercy, of whatever kind. The second: the word of mercy—if I cannot carry out a work of mercy, I will assist by my words. The third: prayer—if I cannot show mercy by deeds or words, I can always do so by prayer. My prayer reaches out even there where I cannot reach out physically. O my Jesus, transform me into Yourself, for You can do all things. (*Diary*, 163)

A Prayer for Mercy on the Whole World:

O greatly merciful God, Infinite Goodness, today all mankind calls out from the abyss of its misery to Your mercy—to Your compassion, O God; and it is with its mighty voice of misery that it cries out. Gracious God, do not reject the prayer of this earth's exiles! O Lord, Goodness beyond our understanding, Who are acquainted with our misery through and through, and know that by our own power we cannot ascend to You, we implore You: anticipate us with Your grace and keep on increasing Your mercy in us, that we may faithfully do Your holy will all through our life and at death's hour. Let the omnipotence of Your mercy shield us from the darts of our salvation's enemies, that we may with confidence, as Your children, await Your final coming—that day known

to You alone. And we expect to obtain everything promised us by Jesus in spite of all our wretchedness. For
Jesus is our Hope: Through His merciful Heart, as
through an open gate, we pass through to heaven.
(*Diary*, 1570)

Chronology of Events

The main events of the life of St. Faustina Kowalska and the steps to her canonization:

August 25, 1905: Sr. Faustina is born Helen Kowalska in the village of Glogowiec, near Lodz, Poland.

1912: At the age of seven, Helen hears for the first time a voice in her soul, calling her to a more perfect way of life.

June 19–25, 1925: At the age of twenty, during the Octave of Corpus Christi, Helen makes a vow of perpetual chastity.

August 1, 1925: Helen is accepted into the Congregation of the Sisters of Our Lady of Mercy as a lay sister. She begins her postulancy at Warsaw and then leaves for Krakow to complete it.

April 30, 1926: Helen begins her two-year novitiate in Krakow, receiving her religious habit and the name Maria Faustina.

February 22, 1931: Sr. Faustina sees the Lord Jesus dressed in a white robe. Red and pale rays stream forth from the area of His heart. "Paint an image," He tells her, "according to the pattern you see, bearing the signature, 'Jesus, I trust in You.'"

January 2, 1934: Sr. Faustina meets with artist Eugene Kazimierowski, who through Fr. Sopocko has been commissioned to paint the image of the Divine Mercy.

June 1934: The Kazimierowski painting is completed. Sr. Faustina is disappointed with it and cries to the Lord, "Who will paint You as beautiful as You are?" In reply, she hears the words, "Not in the beauty of the color nor of the brush lies the greatness of this image, but in My grace" (*Diary*, 313). The painting is hung in the corridor of the Bernardine Sisters' Convent near St. Michael's Church in Vilnius, where Fr. Sopocko is rector.

July 1934: Following the instructions of her spiritual director (Fr. Sopocko), Sr. Faustina begins keeping a personal diary, which she entitles *Divine Mercy in My Soul.*

August 1934: Sr. Faustina suffers a violent attack of asthma for the first time, perhaps already due to tuberculosis, which is to cause her almost constant suffering for the few remaining years of her life.

October 26, 1934: Sr. Faustina sees the Lord Jesus above the chapel in Vilnius, with the same red and pale rays coming from the area of His heart. The rays envelop the chapel and the students' infirmary, and then spread out over the whole world.

April 26–28, 1935: During the celebration concluding the Jubilee Year of the Redemption of the world, the Kazimierowski image of the Divine Mercy is transferred to the Ostra Brama (Shrine of Our Lady of Mercy in Vilnius) and placed in a high window so it may be seen from far away. This event coincides with the second Sunday of Easter, which, according to Sister Faustina, is to be the day of the Feast of Divine Mercy. Father Sopocko delivers a homily about the Divine Mercy.

January 8, 1936: Sr. Faustina visits Bishop Jalbrzykowski and tells him that Jesus has asked for a new congregation to be founded.

October 5, 1936: Fr. Sopocko writes to Sr. Faustina, asking for the texts of the chaplet and the novena to the Divine Mercy.

December 9, 1936: With her health deteriorating, Sr. Faustina is sent to the hospital in Pradnik, a sanatorium in Krakow for tuberculosis patients. Except for a few days during the Christmas holidays, she remains there until March 27, 1937.

December 13, 1936: Under the appearance of her confessor, Jesus Himself hears Sr. Faustina's confession.

April 4, 1937: Fr. Sopocko publishes an article on the Divine Mercy in the *Vilnius Catholic Weekly.*

April 4, 1937: By permission of Archbishop Romuald Jalbrzykowski, the Kazimierowski image is blessed and placed in St. Michael's Church in Vilnius.

September 27, 1937: Sr. Faustina and Mother Irene meet with the printer who is to print holy cards bearing the image of The Divine Mercy.

November 1937: Through the efforts of Fr. Sopocko, the litany, chaplet, and novena to the Divine Mercy are published by the J. Cebulski Press in Krakow in a pamphlet entitled *Christ, King of Mercy.* On the cover of the pamphlet is a color picture representing the merciful Christ with the signature, "Jesus, I trust in You." Holy cards, bearing a copy of Kazimierowski's image of the Divine Mercy on the front and the chaplet on the back, are also printed by Cebulski.

November 10, 1937: Sr. Faustina and Mother Superior Irene look over the pamphlet containing the litany, chaplet, and novena, and the Lord tells Sr. Faustina that many souls have already been drawn to Him through the image.

April 21, 1938: Suffering greatly from tuberculosis, Sr. Faustina leaves the convent for her final five-month stay at the sanatorium in Pradnik.

April 22–May 6, 1938: For fourteen days, at the sanatorium in Pradnik, Sr. Faustina receives Holy Communion from a seraph.

June 24, 1938: Sr. Faustina sees the Sacred Heart of Jesus in the sky in the midst of a great brilliance, the rays streaming from the wound in His side and spreading out over the entire world.

June 1938: She stops writing the diary.

September 2, 1938: Fr. Sopocko visits her at the sanatorium in Pradnik and discovers her in ecstasy.

September 26, 1938: Fr. Sopocko visits her in Krakow for the last time and notes that "she looked like an unearthly being.... I no longer had the slightest doubt that what she had written in her diary about receiving Holy Communion from an angel was really true."

October 5, 1938: At 10:45 P.M., Sr. Faustina dies of multiple tuberculosis in Krakow, at the age of 33.

October 7, 1938: Her funeral coincides with the First Friday of the month and the Feast of Our Lady of the Rosary.

September 1, 1939: German tanks and planes cross the Polish frontier, and the Nazis take control of Poland. In the course of the war, the city of Warsaw, along with many other Polish cities and towns, is destroyed by incendiary and demolition bombs, an apparent fulfillment of Sr. Faustina's earlier prophecy:

> One day Jesus told me that He would cause a chastisement to fall upon the most beautiful city in our country [probably Warsaw]. This chastisement would be that with which God had punished Sodom and Gomorrah. (*Diary, 39*)

Spring 1940: Fr. Joseph Jarzebowski, a Marian priest from Warsaw who had been blacklisted by the Nazi SS, hears about the devotion to the Divine Mercy at a camp in Vilkomir, Lithuania.

July–September 1940: Fr. Jarzebowski prays to the Divine Mercy to help him escape to America.

February 25, 1941: Hearing of Fr. Jarzebowski's plan to escape, Fr. Sopocko gives him a Latin memorandum outlining the devotion to the Divine Mercy. Fr. Jarzebowski promises to do his best to keep the memorandum safe and have it printed when he reaches America. Entrusting himself and his mission to the Divine Mercy, he vows to spend the rest of his life spreading the mercy message and devotion if he reaches safety.

February 26, 1941: Carrying a picture of the merciful Jesus next to his heart and Fr. Sopocko's Divine Mercy memorandum in his traveling bag, Fr. Jarzebowski leaves his hiding place in Vilnius and boards an ordinary trans-Siberian train. Traveling across the whole of Russia and Siberia, he reaches Vladivostock, where the customs officer searches everything except the bag containing the memorandum. No one seems to notice that his American visa is obsolete and invalid, and he is granted Japanese transit.

When he reaches Japan, he finds $30.00 and a ticket to the United States waiting for him, sent by Fr. Joseph Luniewski of the Marians in America. The Polish embassy validates his American visa, and he leaves for America.

May 1941: Fr. Jarzebowski lands on American soil. Full of gratitude for the mercy of God, and remembering his promises to Fr. Sopocko, he begins to share the message of mercy privately and tries to spread the devotion to the Divine Mercy. At a Detroit printery, the first sample copies of the image are made.

June 1941: Asked to assist as confessor at the annual retreat for the Felician Sisters in Enfield, Connecticut, Fr. Jarzebowski speaks to the sisters about the revelations to Sr. Faustina and the essence of devotion to the Divine Mercy, mentioning the special graces given to him. The sisters make a copy of his brief account, and the provincial superior donates a sum of money to have several hundred copies of the image printed.

1941: At a "house meeting" in Washington, D.C., a tiny group of Marians decide to undertake as an apostolate the spreading of the message of devotion to the Divine Mercy, and they begin printing the first novena leaflets.

November 28, 1958: Sr. Faustina's prophecy about the apparent destruction of the devotion to the Divine Mercy (*Diary,* 378 and 1659) begins its fulfillment by a decree of condemnation due to incorrect translation in the Italian version of her diary. The severe ban is mitigated by Pope John XXIII on March 6, 1959, to a "Notification" prohibiting "the spreading of the devotion according to St. Faustina."

October 21, 1965: In the archdiocese of Krakow, twenty-seven years after the death of Faustina, Bishop Julian Groblicki, specially delegated by Archbishop Karol Wojtyla, begins the Informative Process relating to the life and virtues of Sr. Faustina. From this moment, Sr. Faustina is worthy of the title "Servant of God."

November 25, 1966: While the Informative Process relating to the virtues, writings, and devotion of the Servant of God Sr. Faustina is being conducted (October 21, 1965 to September 20, 1967), her remains are exhumed and translated to a tomb specially prepared for this purpose in the chapel of the Sister of Our Lady of Mercy in Lagiewniki. Over the tomb is a black slab with a cross in the center. The slab usually has fresh flowers brought by the faithful, who plead for numerous graces through her intercession.

June 26, 1967: Archbishop Karol Wojtyla becomes Karol Cardinal Wojtyla.

September 20, 1967: The archbishop of Krakow, Karol Cardinal Wojtyla, officially closes the first informative stage in the process for the beatification of the Servant of God Sr. Faustina Kowalska.

January 31, 1968: By a decree of the Sacred Congregation for the Causes of Saints, the Process of Beatification of the Servant of God Sr. Faustina H. Kowalska is formally inaugurated.

April 15, 1978: In response to inquiries from Poland, and in particular Cardinal Wojtyla, about the "Notification" of 1959, the Sacred Congregation for the Canonization of Saints declares the Notification is no longer binding due to the changed circumstances and the opinion of many Polish ordinaries.

October 16, 1978: Karol Cardinal Wojtyla becomes Pope John Paul II.

November 30, 1980: Pope John Paul II publishes his encyclical letter *Rich in Mercy,* in which he stresses that Jesus Christ has revealed God, who is rich in mercy, as Father. He speaks of mercy as "the most stupendous attribute of the Creator and Redeemer" (13).

June 19, 1981: The Sacred Congregation for the Causes of Saints, having completed the investigation of all available writings of the Servant of God Sr. Faustina, issues a decree stating that "nothing stands in the way of proceeding further" with her cause.

October 8, 1981: The Sacred Congregation for the Sacraments and Divine Worship issues a decree confirming the Latin text of a Votive Mass of the Divine Mercy for the Metropolitan Archdiocese of Krakow, Poland.

April 10, 1991: Pope John Paul II, at his general audience, speaks about Sr. Faustina, showing his great respect for her, relating her to his encyclical *Rich in Mercy,* and emphasizing her role in bringing the message of mercy to the world.

March 7, 1992: In the presence of the Holy Father, the Congregation for the Causes of Saints promulgates the Decree of Heroic Virtues, by which the Church acknowledges that Sr. Faustina practiced all the Christian virtues to a heroic degree. As a result, she receives the title "Venerable" Servant of God, and the way is opened for verification of the miracle attributed to her intercession.

In that same year, the healing of Maureen Digan at the tomb of Sr. Faustina is recognized as a miracle by three separate panels appointed by the Sacred Congregation: first a panel of doctors, then of theologians, and finally, of cardinals and bishops.

December 21, 1992: The Holy Father publishes the Church's acceptance of the miracle as granted through the intercession of Sr. Faustina and announces the date for her solemn beatification.

April 18, 1993: Sr. Faustina is beatified in Rome on the Second Sunday of Easter (which Our Lord had revealed to her as the "Feast of Divine Mercy").

September 4, 1993: John Paul II prays the rosary at the Shrine of Our Lady of Mercy, Ostra Brama, in Vilnius, Lithuania, where the Image of the Merciful Jesus was first displayed.

September 5, 1993: John Paul II kneels and prays at the Image of the Divine Mercy, painted under the direction of Sr. Faustina, in the Church of the Holy Spirit, Vilnius.

January 23, 1995: Pope John Paul II grants to the Polish bishops that the Sunday after Easter be the Sunday of Divine Mercy because of the need and desire of the faithful.

April 23, 1995: Pope John Paul II celebrates Divine Mercy Sunday in Holy Spirit Church, the Shrine of Divine Mercy in Rome (*L'Osservatore Romano,* English Edition, April 26, 1995). In his homily, he challenges us to "trust in the Lord and be Apostles of Divine Mercy."

In his "Regina Caeli" address, he speaks of this Sunday as the day of thanksgiving for God's mercy, called the Sunday of Divine Mercy. He challenges us to personally *experience* this mercy in order to be merciful and forgive—and so break the spiral of violence by the miracle of forgiveness.

June 7, 1997: Pope John Paul II makes a pilgrimage to the Shrine of Divine Mercy in Lagiewniki (Krakow), Poland, at the convent where the relics of Sr. Faustina are honored.

November 20, 1999: Pope John Paul II accepts the healing of the heart of Fr. Ronald Pytel of Baltimore, Maryland, as the miracle for the canonization of Sr. Faustina.

April 30, 2000: Pope John Paul II canonizes St. Faustina Kowalska and proclaims Divine Mercy Sunday for the universal Church.

Bibliography:
Recommended Materials on St. Faustina
and the Divine Mercy

The codes for materials from the Marian Helpers are included in boldface to make ordering easier.

Resources available from the Marian Helpers Center
Stockbridge, MA   01263, U.S.A.

The Life of Faustina Kowalska.* Sr. Sophia Michalenko, C.M.G.T.
A chronological presentation of the life of St. Faustina as observed through her diary. (The life of Faustina Kowalska was an invaluable resource in the writing of *Meet Saint Faustina*.)
DML6 256 pp. $13.00

Beginning Materials on Divine Mercy

Leaflets and cards:
The Message of Mercy - **FYDM**
The Message of Mercy Flyer - **MPL**
The Message of Divine Mercy - **MDS**
Divine Mercy Image card with **Chaplet** - **MPC**
Beginners, ask for a sample of free Divine Mercy leaflets sent out by Marian Helpers - **DMPK1**

Books:

   Divine Mercy Message and Devotion - **M17**
   Now Is the Time for Mercy - **NTM**

Video:

   Divine Mercy No Escape - **DMVC**, use anytime.

Materials for Continued Reading

Books:

   The Life of St. Faustina Kowalska - **DML6**
   The Diary of St. Faustina, Divine Mercy in My Soul - **NBFD**

For Further Growth

Encyclicals:

Rich in Mercy (Dives in Misericordia). Encyclical of John
   Paul II on Divine Mercy.

Books:

The Diary of St. M. Faustina Kowalska: *Divine Mercy in My
   Soul.* The newest edition, describing her revelations of Jesus
   as the Divine Mercy. Includes a preface and up-to-date
   information on the Marians and the Sisters of Our Lady of
   Mercy, two religious congregations that promote the message of mercy. Digest size. 697 pages, including a 24-page
   color photo section.

BFDS (Spanish)	$15.00
NBFD	$14.00

Faustina: Apostle of Divine Mercy. Catherine Odell.
Available from Our Sunday Visitor, Huntington, IN 46750.

Now Is the Time for Mercy. Rev. George W. Kosicki, C.S.B.
A concise handbook to the Divine Mercy message and
devotion.
NTM 104 pp. $8.00

Study Guide to the Diary of St. Faustina Kowalska. Rev.
George W. Kosicki, C.S.B. An index of 90 topics; a com-
prehensive reference tool.
SGD 159 pp. $14.95

Tell My Priests. Rev. George W. Kosicki, C.S.B. A guide to
the Divine Mercy message and devotion written by a priest
for priests. Helpful to laity, too.
DML9 124 pp. $8.50

Young Life of Sister Faustina. Introduces middle-school-age
readers to this saint.
YLSF 109 pp., 19 illustrations $7.95

Helen's Special Picture. Written and illustrated by Dave
Previtali. Introduces young children to Sr. Faustina.
Wonderfully expressive color drawings accompany a simple
text, which captures the drama of Faustina's life and mission.
HSPB 32 pp., 15 color illustrations $7.50

Booklets:

The Divine Mercy Message and Devotion. English edition of
the devotion booklet with Chaplet, Novena, and selected
prayers. Pocket size (3 1/2 by 6) with clear plastic protective cover.
M17 92 pp. $4.00

Foreign Language Devotion Booklets. With chaplet, novena,
and prayers. With clear plastic protective cover.
PM17 (Polish) 80 pp. $2.00
M17S (Spanish) 32 pp. $4.00
M17Port (Portuguese) 37 pp. $4.00

Conversations With the Merciful Lord. Rev. George W.
Kosicki, C.S.B. Moving conversations between the Merciful
Savior and five kinds of souls: sinful, despairing, suffering,
striving, and perfect. All taken from the diary of St. Faustina.
BKC 32 pp. $3.25

Come to My Mercy. Rev. George W. Kosicki, C.S.B. A complete
step-by-step instruction manual for how to give and receive
mercy.
DML12 32 pp. $3.25

Praying With Sister Faustina. Colleen Free. Both those who are new to the message of Divine Mercy and those long attached to it will appreciate this booklet. Colleen Free has gathered brief prayers from Sr. Faustina's diary and grouped them according to subjects like "Love of God" and "Night Prayer." It is suited to the hectic life we all face.
PWSF 69 pp., plastic cover $3.25

The Divine Mercy Prayerbook: The Chaplet of Divine Mercy for the Sick and Dying During Adoration. A great resource for those who minister to the dying.
DMPBA 40 pp., 5 b/w illustrations $3.25

O Blessed Host, Have Mercy on Us! This newest booklet by Fr. George W. Kosicki, C.S.B., provides more than eighty excerpts on the Eucharist from Sr. Faustina's diary. Ideal for use before or after Holy Mass or in adoration.
OBH 64 pp., plastic cover $3.25

Catalog:
The National Shrine of the Divine Mercy: CL. A booklet describing the special services offered by the Association of Marian Helpers, materials on Divine Mercy and Mary, enrollment cards, and various other materials, and listing the various images of the Divine Mercy.

Video Tapes:

Divine Mercy—No Escape. The moving story of the young Polish nun chosen by God to share His message of mercy with the world. Revised for prayer groups, schools, churches, and Apostles of Divine Mercy programs. Narrated by Helen Hayes, 47 min.
DMVC $14.95

Time for Mercy. This award-winning video explores signs of God's mercy in our time. It takes an unflinching look at the biblical witness of God's judgment and mercy, the offer of God's mercy in Christ, and the troubles of today's world— from recurring natural disasters and environmental threats to the growing list of human tragedies. Narrated by actor Joseph Campanella. 1 hour, VHS.
TMV $14.95

Sr. Faustina: The Apostle of Divine Mercy. The story of Helen Kowalska who, as Sr. Faustina, became the Apostle of Divine Mercy. Filmed in Rome, Warsaw, Czestochowa, and her birthplace, Swinice, Poland. Includes on-site interviews with those who knew her. 1 hour.
LSF $30.00

Audiotape Album:

New Heart, New Spirit. The audio portion of the television retreat on Divine Mercy by Fr. Harold Cohen, SJ, Fr. George W. Kosicki, CSB, Fr. Seraphim Michalenko, MIC, and Vinny Flynn. Thirteen half hour tapes.

Available from: Closer Walk Ministries, P.O. Box 50860, New Orleans, LA   70150-0860; Phone: 504-834-4200

Divine Mercy Music:

The Chaplet of Divine Mercy. Recorded in the National Shrine of the Divine Mercy in Stockbridge, Massachusetts, by Still Waters and Friends. The chaplet features the traditional melody used by the Sisters of Our Lady of Mercy at St. Faustina's convent in Poland. Since the chaplet is recorded on both sides of the tape, no rewinding is necessary. 40 min.

ADC (cassette)	$10.00
CSM (sheet music)	$4.00
CCD (compact disc)	$14.00

Heal Us, Lord: Songs of Mercy. Meditative songs of mercy and healing, including original compositions based on the diary of St. Faustina. With its gentle blend of old and new hymns, this tape creates a soothing atmosphere for prayer, reflection, or quiet healing time. Sung by Still Waters. 45 min.

Available from: Spirit Song Ministries, P.O. Box 486, Stockbridge, MA 01262